S

COMPLETE CANON USER'S GUIDE

CANON
EOS 50/E - *Elan II/E*

HOVE FOTO BOOKS

Philip Raby

In North America the Canon EOS 50/50E is known as the Canon EOS Elan II/Elan IIE

All text, illustrations and data apply to cameras with either name.

First English Edition November 1995
Reprinted May 1997
Reprinted May 1999
Published by Hove Foto Books

Newpro UK Limited
Old Sawmills Road, Faringdon, Oxon.
SN7 7DS, England
Tel: (01367) 242411 Fax: (01367) 241124

Typeset and produced by William J Anthony Partnership Limited
Newlands Building, Lowlands, Vale, Guernsey, Channel Islands GY3 5XJ

Printed by
Wincanton Press Co. Ltd., Great Britain

British Library Cataloguing-in-Publication Data
A catalogue record for this book is available from the British Library

Raby Philip -
Canon EOS 50/50E - Elan II/E

ISBN : 1-874031-59-2

Worldwide Distribution:

Newpro UK Ltd.,
Old Sawmills Road, Faringdon, Oxon.,
SN7 7DS, England
Tel: (01367) 242411 Fax: (01367) 241124

The author would like to thank Canon Inc. for their assistance and permission for the use of illustrations and drawings.

Contents

Page No.

1. Introduction 11
   A brief history of Canon 11
   What this book will do for you 12
   Model names 13

2. Finding your way around 14
   The anatomy of your camera 14
   LCD panel 23
   Viewfinder 24
   The beep 24

3. Getting your EOS ready for action 26
   Installing the battery 26
   Checking the battery 26
   Maximising battery life 28
   Attaching the lens 28
   The neck strap 29
   Loading a film 30
   Film speed 31
   Infrared film 32

4. Full Auto and PIC modes 33
   Full Auto 33
   Portrait 35
   Landscape 35
   Sport 36
   Close-up 37

5. Creative Zone modes 39
   Program 39
   Program Shift 40
   Shutter Priority 41
   Aperture Priority 42
   Manual 43
   Bulb 46

6. Depth-of-field 48
What is depth-of-field? 48
Focusing and depth-of-field..48
Depth-of-field Preview..61
Depth-of-field the lazy way..62

7. Metering modes..63
Evaluative..63
Centre-weighted Average 64
Partial 65
Stop-down 66
AE Lock..66

8. Exposure Compensation 68
How to set Exposure Compensation..68
When to use Exposure Compensation..69
Auto Exposure Bracketing (AEB) 70
Combining AEB and Exposure Compensation 71

9. More about focusing..72
One shot..72
AI Servo 72
Predictive focusing..73
AI Focus 73
Manual Focus..73
Limits to Autofocus..74

10. Multipoint focusing..76
Automatic point selection 76
Manual point selection 77
Eye-control selection..77

11. Film winding and rewinding..81
Single exposure 81
Continuous exposure 82
Film rewind..82

12. Multiple Exposures 84
Setting Multiple Exposure mode 84
Using Multiple Exposure mode 85
What is Multiple Exposure mode for? 86

13. Custom Functions 88
Using Custom Functions 88
Setting Custom Functions 88

14. Basic flash photography 93
What is TTL flash metering? 93
Using the built-in flash 94
Red-eye and the built-in flash 96
Red-eye reduction lamp 97
Other ways of avoiding red-eye 97
Using a Speedlite 99
Macro Ring Lite ML-3 102

15. Using flash 104
Flash in different shooting modes 104
Flash Exposure Compensation 106
Combining Flash & Ambient Exposure Comp. 107

16. Using your EOS with studio flash 109

17. Self-timer operation 112
Setting the self-timer 112
Using the self-timer 112
Eyepiece cover 113
Using the self-timer to avoid camera shake 114

18. Quartz Date models 115
How the Quartz Date back works 115
Setting the Quartz Date back 115
Using the Quartz Date back 116
Replacing the Quartz Date back battery 117

19. EF lenses 118
Why buy a Canon lens? 118
Lens motors 119
Focal length 120
Maximum aperture 120
Prime and zoom lenses 131
L Series lenses 132
Wide-angle prime lenses 132
Standard lenses 133
Short telephoto lenses 134
Medium telephoto lenses 135
Super-telephoto lenses 136
Wide-angle and standard zoom lenses 138
Telephoto zoom lenses 142
Tilt-and-shift lenses 145
Macro lenses 146

20. Accessories for your EOS 50/E – Elan II/E 148
Battery Pack BP-50 148
Battery Pack BP-5 150
Remote Control RC-1 150
Remote Switch RS-60E3 152
Extension Tubes 152
Extenders 152
Close-up lenses 153
Lens hoods 153
Dioptric correction lenses 153
Camera case 154

21. Jargon buster 155

22. Specifications 166

Foreword – out with the old

Who said that modern electronic cameras do not take better photographs? I had my first camera when I was six years old – a Kodak Box Brownie. No, I'm not that old, it was a hand-me-down from my father.

The Box Brownie was to camera technology what the Model T Ford was to car design – simple, cheap and very popular. Unfortunately, the camera did nothing to help its user take good photographs. And at such a tender age, I knew more about building Lego houses than taking photographs.

The combination of my ignorance and the camera's elemental controls led to an usually high failure rate. One problem was that if I forgot to wind the film on, the shutter would still fire, so multiple exposures were common. No built-in motordrives here – I had to turn a knob on the side of the camera until the next frame number appeared in a little red window. Out of a roll of eight frames, I would be delighted to get two photographs with a recognisable image on. Now you may think that this would have put me off photography for life and led me to pursue a career as an accountant, or maybe a lion-tamer. But no, I didn't know any better and for years thought that taking a good photograph was about as likely as flared trousers going out of fashion.

A few years after, I graduated to a slightly more modern Kodak Folding Brownie. My father gave it to me to take on a school trip to France. Before embarking on this, my first trip overseas, I received a brief lesson on apertures and shutter speeds: "One sixtieth of a second at f8 should cope with most conditions." Surprisingly, I came back with a few decent snaps of Normandy, but there were still a fair number of failures.

I struggled on with the Folding Brownie until I saved up to buy my first 35mm camera – a second-hand Zorki 4. This tough little Russian Leica copy was a super camera that boasted rangefinder focusing. Unfortunately, it wasn't until I started to use the camera that I realised that It lacked an exposure meter, so I invested in a single hand-held model – also from somewhere behind the old Iron Curtain.

As I learned more about photography, my success rate improved, although the Zorki did little to help and I stuck to my belief that photography was a hit-and-miss affair. And then I discovered Canon EOS cameras. For the first time, 36 out of 36 frames were correctly exposed and focused. This was a real revelation. What's more, I gave an EOS 50/E – Elan II/E, set to Full Auto mode, to a six year old, and the photographs he took were surprisingly good - no multiple exposures there!

What happened to my earlier cameras? The Box Brownie has disappeared without trace, but the Folding Brownie and Zorki 4 look very nice on my living room shelves. And that's how they will remain – as ornaments. After all, who would drive around in a Model T Ford, when a modern car takes you from 0-60mph in seven seconds in air-conditioned comfort?

This book is dedicated to my wife Janet

Acknowledgments

Thanks are due to:

My wife, Janet Raby, for proofreading.

Daniel Lezano, of Canon UK Helpline, for more proofreading.

Robert Scott, Publisher of EOS magazine and Canon User, for the loan of an Apple Macintosh computer.

Chris Coleman of Newpro UK Limited.

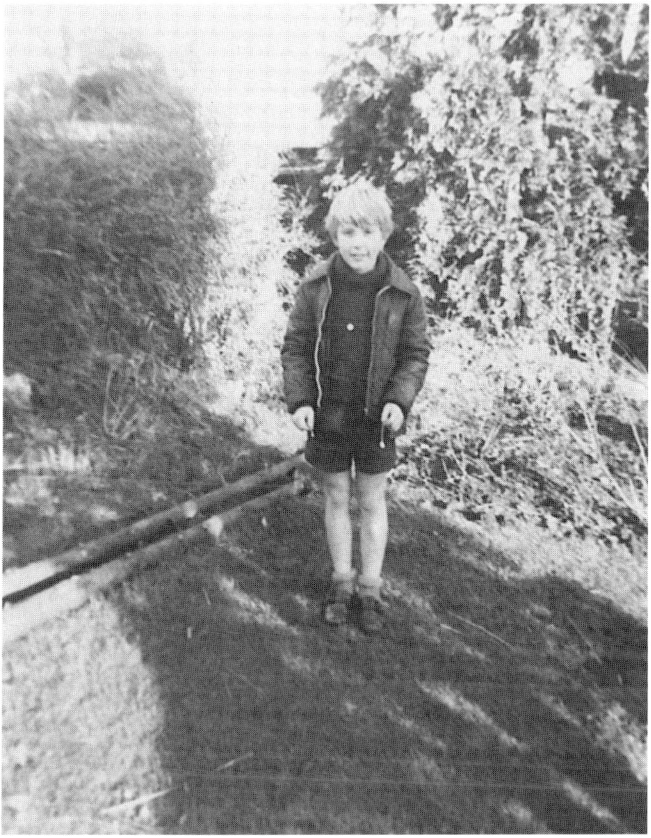

The author photographed by his Box Brownie, circa 1970.

Photograph: Herbert Raby

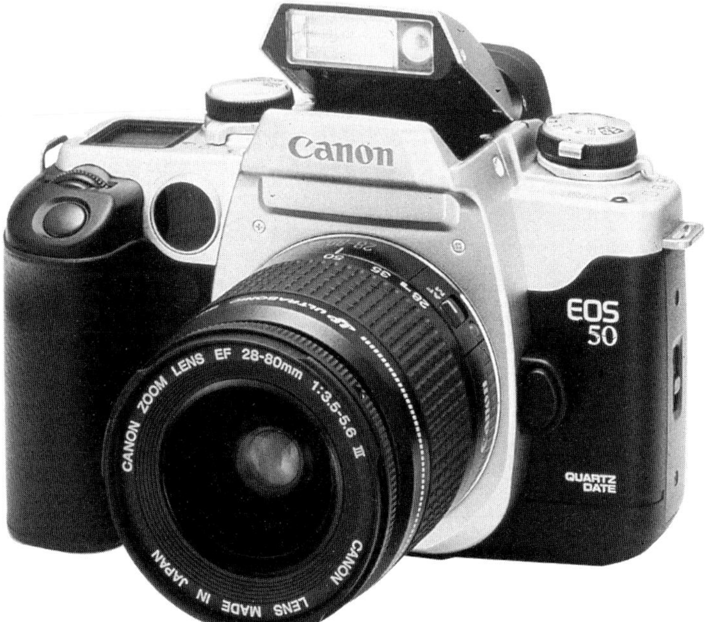

The Canon EOS 50 - *Elan II*

Chapter One
Introduction

A brief history of Canon

Congratulations on buying a Canon EOS 50/E – Elan II/E. You have bought a camera with an enviable heritage. The origins of Canon date back to the 1930s, when two Japanese entrepreneurs decided to build a 35mm rangefinder camera that would compete with the finest European models.

Their first prototypes were called Kwannons, of which there is only one surviving example. The brand was named after a Buddhist deity, but was changed to Canon in 1935 to avoid offending religious groups and to be more appealing to western buyers. The two names are pronounced identically in Japan.

The early Canons were rangefinder models and owed their styling to the popular Leica models of the day. The first Canon SLR camera was introduced in 1959. SLR stands for Single Lens Reflex and means that the viewfinder image is formed from light passing through the lens, so what you see in the viewfinder is the image that forms on the film during exposure. Your EOS 50/E – Elan II/E is an SLR design.

A series of Canon SLR cameras was produced during the 1950s and 1960s. In the 1970s, Canon started to produce cameras that used electronics to control the exposure and shutter system. This was a revolution that led to the world beating AE-1 of 1976. This remarkable camera was an instant hit and became a best-seller. It was followed by the even more successful A-1, which introduced many features now found in your EOS 50/E – Elan II/E, such as Shutter Priority, Aperture Priority and Program modes, and a LED viewfinder read-out that lets you see the set shutter speed and aperture without taking your eye away from the camera.

These features were later incorporated into the futuristic – and now classic – Canon T90, which turned camera design upside down with its smooth, ergonomic curves.

The T90 led the way for the first EOS – the EOS 650. Introduced in 1987, this camera was a gamble for Canon because it used a totally new lens mount system that was not compatible with earlier Canon cameras and lenses. The reason for the new mount was that the camera featured a revolutionary autofocus system that relied on a focus motor in the lens. Other manufacturers were developing autofocus cameras with motors in the body, but Canon's engineers decided that this was a compromise and would not give the fast, accurate focusing that top photographers demanded.

Canon's gamble paid off. There have now been over 20 EOS models and they have become the most popular SLR cameras in the world.

By the way, in case you're wondering, EOS stands for Electro Optical System. And Eos was the Greek goddess of dawn, daughter of Helios and mother of Memnon.

The EOS 50 – Elan II and EOS 50E – Elan IIE were launched in August 1995. They are mid-range EOS cameras which replaced the extremely popular EOS 100 (Elan).

The only difference between the two cameras is that the EOS 50E – Elan IIE features Eye-control focus. They break with tradition by being the first EOS models that are not completely black or grey. The upper body is clad in 1mm thick titanium-effect aluminium, which gives the camera a solid, traditional feel. What's more, the EOS 50/E – Elan II/E has two Command Dials that allow you to set most camera functions quickly and easily – other EOS models rely more on buttons, which are considered by some people to be fiddly and less positive.

What this book will do for you

This book is a detailed guide to the EOS 50/E – Elan II/E and its accessories; it is not a general guide to photography. However, when read in conjunction with the camera instruction book, it will help you to understand fully the operation of this fascinating camera. In turn, that will enable you to take better photographs.

Model names

The EOS 50 and EOS 50E are identical apart from the Eye-control feature of the latter. Therefore, throughout this book the cameras are referred to as EOS 50/E except when referring to specific models.

The cameras have different names in North America to the rest of the world. The EOS 50 is known as the EOS Elan II, and the EOS 50E, the EOS Elan IIE. Throughout the book the North American names are given after the international names.

Quartz Date (QD) versions of the cameras are available. Except where specifically referred to, these cameras are identical to the non-QD versions.

Chapter Two

Finding your way around

The EOS 50/E – Elan II/E is designed to be simple and straightforward to use. However, to get the very best from your camera you should get to know it so well that it becomes an extension of your hands – nothing should come between you and your photography – not even a camera!

The best way to learn the camera's controls is to use them, but you can give yourself a head start by reading this chapter and trying out all the features in the comfort of your home.

Each camera feature is briefly described and, where relevant, includes a chapter reference (see diagram 1 and 2).

1. Built-in flash

The EOS 50/E – Elan II/E has a handy built-in flash unit. This pops up automatically when required in Full-Auto and some PIC modes. In Creative Zone modes, it can be activated manually when required by pressing the Flash button.

Chapter 14

2. Flash button

Press this button to activate the built-in flash in Creative Zone modes.

Chapter 14

3. Second Command Dial

Turn this to set the Autofocus mode. It has three positions – One Shot, AI Focus and AI Servo.

Chapter 9

4. LCD panel

This small panel displays a wealth of information about camera settings. See the diagram on page 23 for a full description. LCD stands for Liquid Crystal Display. After many years of use it is possible that the panel will fade and

Diagram 1
The Camera Front

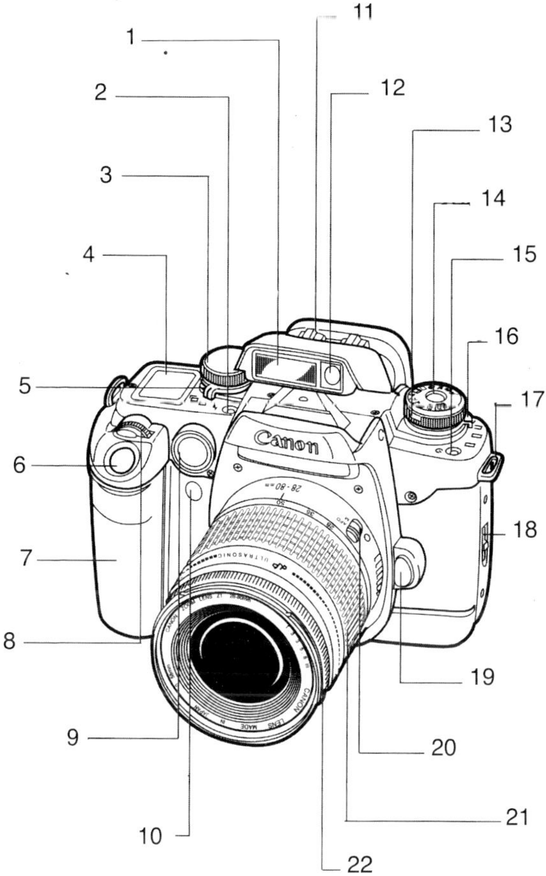

become hard to read. If this happens, return the camera to a Canon Authorised Service Centre to have the LCD panel replaced.

5. Film Advance Mode lever

This lever sets the film winding mode: choose from Single Frame or Continuous. A pointer indicates which setting has been made.

Chapter 11

6. Shutter release button

No camera would be complete without a shutter button. The one on your EOS 50/E – Elan II/E has two steps. Press it half-way to activate autofocus and exposure metering. Press it all the way to fire the shutter and advance the film onto the next frame. It is not possible to use the shutter button when the main Command Dial is set to Lock (L) or when the lens is unable to focus in One Shot mode.

When the shutter button is pressed halfway, the viewfinder display and LCD panel are activated. The display remains on for four seconds after releasing the shutter button.

To avoid camera shake spoiling your photographs, press the shutter button firmly but gently, taking care not to shake the camera.

7. Hand grip

Not only does this grip make the EOS 50/E – Elan II/E easy and comfortable to hold, it also houses the 2CR5 battery that powers the camera.

Chapter 3

8. Electronic Input Dial

This simple-to-use dial is operated by your right-hand index finger. Depending on the shooting mode the camera is in, the Electronic Input Dial is used to set the shutter speed, aperture, control Program Shift and much more. It turns in both directions and the settings made appear in the LCD panel and viewfinder display.

9. Auxiliary Focus Light and Self-timer lamp

In low light, this lamp illuminates the subject to help the camera to 'see' what it is focusing on. The light has a limited range, so do not expect it to work with subjects more than about six feet away.

During Self-timer operation, the light flashes twice a second for the first eight seconds of the countdown, and then increases in speed to eight flashes a second for the last two seconds before the shutter fires.

Chapter 17

10. Wireless Remote Control Sensor

This sensor receives signals from the optional Remote Controller RC-1.

Chapter 20

11. Hotshoe

This allows a dedicated Speedlite flashgun to be attached to the camera. The hotshoe has a number of electrical contacts that allow the camera and Speedlite to communicate with each other during TTL, A-TTL and E-TTL flash photography.

The hotshoe also accepts other accessories, including an off-camera flash lead, remote control receptor or a hotshoe/PC adaptor for connecting the camera to studio flash units. Another handy accessory that fits onto the hotshoe is a mini spirit level (available from photo dealers) for checking that the camera is horizontal.

Chapter 14

12. Red-eye Reduction lamp

Photographs of people with glaring red-eyes are annoying and unflattering. When activated, this lamp shines at the subject to make their retinas contract before taking a picture. This reduces the risk of red-eye occurring.

Chapter 14

13. Lock Release button

When the main Command Dial is set to Lock (L), you have to press this button before you can turn the dial to another position. This ensures that the camera cannot be turned on by accident.

14. Main Command Dial

A major control in the camera and a trademark feature that makes EOS cameras so easy to use.

The main Command Dial is used to set the shooting mode – choose from Full Auto, four PIC modes and five Creative Zone modes. The main Command Dial also sets Eye-control calibration (EOS 50E/Elan IIE only) and Custom Function control.

When you are not using your camera, turn the main Command Dial to 'L'. This is the Lock position that turns off the camera and prevents the shutter button being depressed accidentally.

15. Self-timer and Remote Control button

This button activates the self-timer which delays the shutter firing for ten seconds after pressing the shutter button – ideal for self portraits, and for avoiding camera shake during long exposures.

Chapter 17

16. Metering mode lever

This lever lets you set the metering mode. Three settings are available – Evaluative, Centre-weighted Average and Partial. A pointer indicates which setting has been made.

Chapter 7

17. Neck strap lug

There is one of these on each end of the camera for attaching a neck strap. Carrying your camera on a strap around your neck ensures that it is always ready for action and safe from being dropped.

Chapter 3

18. Camera back latch

Slide this latch downwards to open the camera back for loading and unloading film. Before doing so, look through the film window to see if a film is loaded. If there is, check the LCD panel to make sure the film symbol is flashing – this tells you that the film is fully rewound ready for removal. Never operate this catch when you are part-way through a film – the exposed frames will be fogged and you will lose your precious images.

Chapter 3

19. Lens Release button

This button must be pressed before the lens can be removed from the camera.

Chapter 3

20. Focus mode switch

This switch is found on most Canon EF lenses. When it is set to 'AF', autofocus is activated. Slide it to 'M' for manual focusing, in this mode 'M.F' appears in the LCD panel to warn you that autofocus is disabled.

Chapter 9

21. Zoom ring

Only found on Canon EF zoom lenses, turn this ring to set the lens focal length to suit the subject.

Chapter 19

22. Focusing ring

Found on some Canon EF lenses, this ring is used for focusing when the Focus mode switch is set to 'M'. If your lens does not have a focusing ring, you have to turn the end of the lens barrel to focus manually.

Chapter 9

23. Viewfinder eyepiece

Look through here to see what you are taking a photograph of. If your eyesight is not perfect, you can fit a dioptre correction lens over the eyepiece to give a sharp image. On the EOS 50E – Elan IIE the viewfinder is surrounded by eight infrared emitting diodes (IREDS), these shine into the eye to determine what focus point you are looking at.

24. Viewfinder eyecup

This removable rubber surround provides a soft surface for your eye to rest against and blocks stray light from entering the viewfinder.

25. Function button

This button is used to set little-used functions. Each time you press it a different function becomes active and is displayed in the LCD panel. The functions set this way are: Manual film speed setting; Auto Exposure Bracketing (AEB); Red-eye Reduction; Sound mode; Multiple Exposures; Flash Compensation.

26. Midroll film rewind button

If you wish to remove a film part-way through, press this button to activate midroll rewind. It is recessed so that you cannot press it by accident.

Chapter 3

27. Film window

This handy feature lets you see at a glance whether or not a film is loaded in your camera. What's more, film manufacturers make sure that the essential information about film (type, speed, length) is printed on its cassette in such a position that it can be read through this window. Get into the habit of looking in here before you open the camera back.

Chapter 3

28. AE Lock, Custom Function and FE Lock button

Press this button to set AE Lock in Creative Zone modes. When using a Speedlite 380EX, it also sets FE Lock. The button is also used for setting Custom Functions when the main Command Dial is at the 'CF' position.

Chapters 7, 13, 15

Diagram 2
The Camera Rear

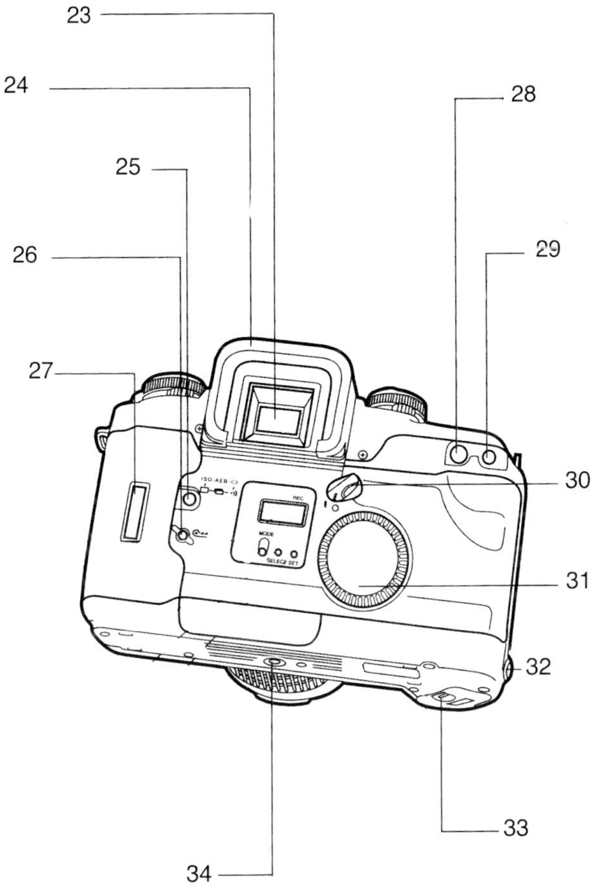

29. Focus point Selector button

This button allows you to manually choose the active focus point. When all three focus points light up, automatic point selection is switched on (or Eye-control – EOS 50E/Elan IIE only).

Chapter 10

30. Quick Control Dial switch

Turn this to '1' to switch on the Quick Control Dial. Turn it to '0' to turn off the Quick Control Dial and lock any settings that have been made with the dial.

31. Quick Control Dial

The Quick Control Dial is used to set Exposure Compensation, Flash Compensation and aperture (Manual mode only). The Quick Control Dial switch must be set to '1' before you can use the dial.

Chapters 8, 15, 5

32. Remote Control socket

Unlike many modern cameras, the EOS 50/E – Elan II/E can be fitted with a remote control shutter release to avoid camera shake during long exposures and to fire the camera from a distance. This 2.5mm jack socket accepts the Canon Remote Switch RS60E3.

Chapter 20

33. Battery Compartment cover

Open this cover to insert the 2CR5 battery that is required to power the camera. Don't forget to always carry a spare battery in case the one in the camera runs down.

Chapter 3

34. Tripod socket

Accepts a standard tripod or monopod screw.

LCD panel

Diagram 3 shows all the information that can be displayed on the LCD panel. You'll never see all the symbols at one time, but it is a good idea to learn what they all mean.

Diagram 3

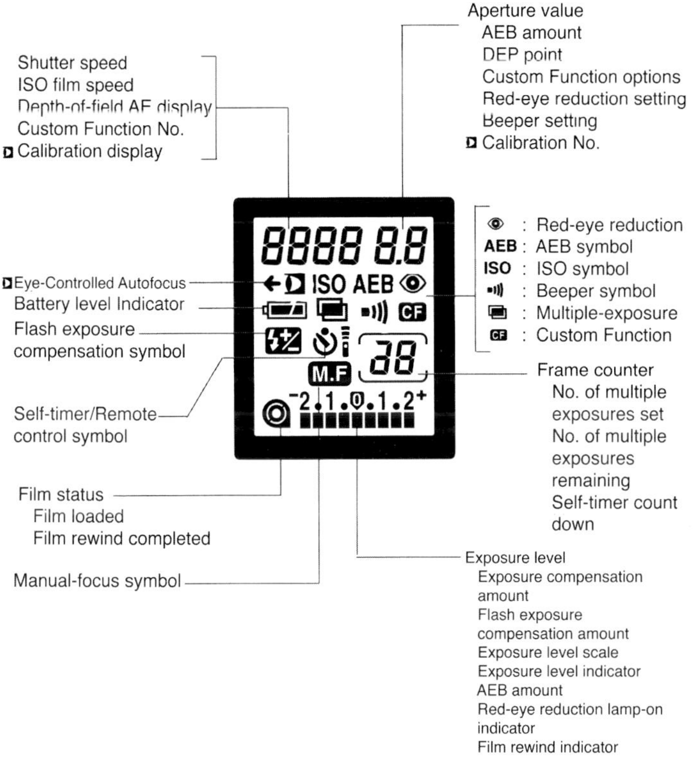

The viewfinder

When you look into the viewfinder of the EOS 50/E – Elan II/E, this is what you see (diagram 4). When you half press the shutter button, the display at the bottom of the viewfinder comes on. It remains active for 4 seconds after the shutter button is released. If the shutter speed reading is blinking, it means that there is not enough light for hand-held photography without the risk of camera shake spoiling the photograph. Mount the camera on a tripod, monopod or other firm surface, or use flash. Your EOS 50/E – Elan II/E uses the rule-of-thumb that says that the shutter speed should be at least 1/focal length for hand-held photography. Therefore, if you are using a short focal length lens, such as 28mm, you can get away with longer shutter speeds than when you are using a telephoto lens.

The beep

You will soon notice that your EOS 50/E – Elan II/E beeps at you from time to time. This is to confirm correct focus – the green in-focus symbol appears in the viewfinder. Although this is very useful, you may find that there are times when the beep is infuriating or intrusive– perhaps during wildlife photography, or at a concert. Because of this, the EOS 50/E – Elan II/E allows you to turn off the beep in Creative Zone modes.

To do this, press the Function Button until the sound symbol and '1' appear in the LCD panel. Now turn the Electronic Input Dial to change the '1' to a '0'. The beep will now remain silent and the sound symbol will disappear from the LCD panel. To turn the beep back on, repeat the procedure and set '1', the sound symbol will return.

The beep sounds during self-timer operation (see Chapter 17). This is also silenced by turning off the beep.

Diagram 4
Viewfinder Information

The viewfinder is shown with all the information displayed.

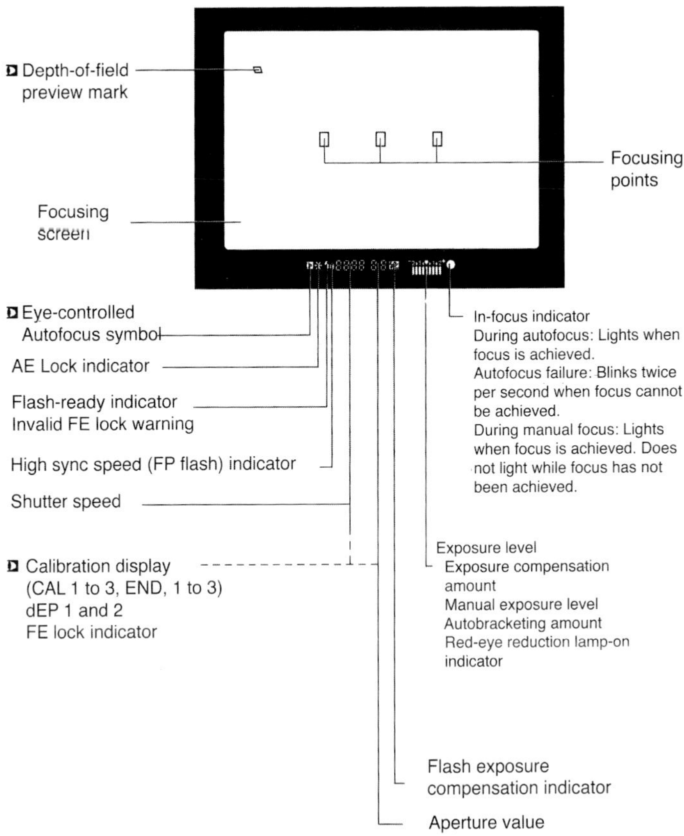

Chapter Three

Getting your EOS ready for action

Before you can go and take photographs with your EOS 50/E – Elan II/E, there are a few essential preparations that you must make to get it ready for action.

Power to your EOS

Your EOS 50/E – Elan II/E contains state-of-the-art electronics. In effect, it is a camera, computer, flashgun and lightmeter all rolled into one. So, not surprisingly, the camera needs electricity for it to work.

The EOS 50/E – Elan II/E is normally powered by a small, but powerful, 6 volt 2CR5 lithium cell. These batteries are not cheap, as you will find out when you go to buy one, but when you consider what it has to power, the compact cell becomes good value for money. Practically every feature of the EOS 50/E – Elan II/E requires power from the battery, for instance; the motordrives to wind and rewind the film, the built-in flashgun and its metering system, the shutter, exposure meter, lens motors to control aperture and focusing, the LCD and viewfinder display, and the camera's microprocessor.

Installing the battery

The battery slips into a compartment in the base of the camera. To get into this, release the catch with your finger nail and open the hinged cover. Make sure that the end of the battery with the contacts on goes in first – the battery will only fit one way, so you can't get it wrong (see diagram 5). Make sure that the cover is firmly closed.

Checking the battery

Your EOS 50/E – Elan II/E will not work if the battery is dead, so it is important to keep an eye on its state. The LCD panel

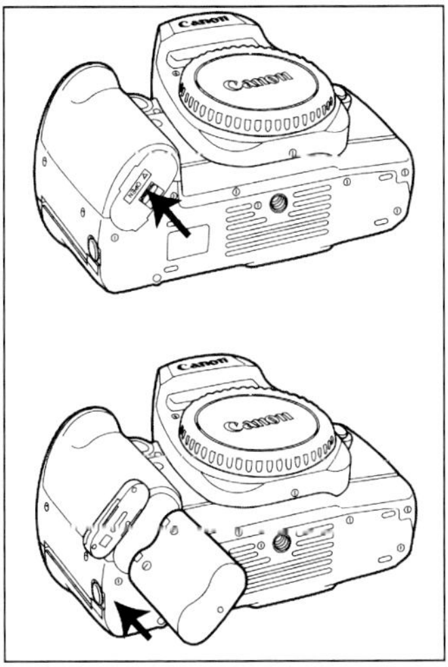

Diagram 5: *Unclip the battery compartment cover with your finger nail and insert the battery as shown.*

displays a battery check indicator; get into the habit of looking at this every time that you use the camera. The indicator is a battery symbol. When it is totally black, the battery is at full power. When only half the symbol is black, the battery is partly used, but still has plenty of life in it. When the symbol is clear, the battery is almost exhausted – be ready to replace it. Eventually, the clear battery symbol will start to flash. This means that – although there is enough power for a correct exposure – film advance and rewind may not occur, neither may there be enough power for the lens to focus.

Do not replace the battery as soon as the indicator becomes clear. As long as a battery has enough life in it to power the camera, you can continue to take photographs. Don't think that a low battery will give incorrect exposures – when the camera senses that battery power is too low, it locks the shutter – you will no longer be able to take a photograph. Then, and not before, is the time to load a fresh battery.

It is a good idea to always carry a spare battery. It is annoying to be stuck with a camera you cannot use, and 2CR5 batteries are not available at every corner shop. But do not keep the same spare for years – batteries deteriorate with age, so always rotate your supplies.

If you are out in very cold conditions, the battery performance will drop. If this happens, remove the battery and warm it against your body before putting it back in the camera.

Maximising battery life

When you first get your EOS 50/E – Elan II/E you will be constantly playing with it, and your friends and family will be keen to have a go too. Even if you are not one to fiddle, you need to spend time getting to know the camera controls. All this uses power, so don't be surprised when your first battery does not last very long; accept it as an essential part of the learning procedure.

Once the novelty has worn off and you know your EOS 50/E – Elan II/E like the back of your hand, its batteries will last a lot longer. If you want to maximise battery life, do not use the built-in flash unnecessarily, avoid activating the viewfinder display and focusing the lens if you do not intend to take a photograph, and use the depth-of-field preview sparingly.

Some people remove the battery from their camera when they are not using it, thinking that will help to conserve it. But, in fact, continuously removing and replacing it can actually decrease battery life. Just remember to switch the camera to Lock before you put it away, otherwise the shutter button may get depressed in your camera case. This will switch on the viewfinder display and drain the battery very quickly.

If you use your camera a lot, or you travel to areas where 2CR5 batteries are hard to find, there are alternative power supplies available – see Chapter 20.

Attaching the lens

Your EOS 50/E – Elan II/E is an interchangeable lens camera. This means that the lens can be removed from it, allowing you to choose one that most suits the type of photograph you are taking – see Chapter 19 for more information on lenses.

You probably bought your camera with a standard zoom lens – with a focal length of 28-80mm or 35-105mm. This is ideal for general photography and, if you do not have another lens, you will have no reason to remove it.

The camera and lens come separately. The lens mount on the front of the camera is protected by a body cap. This is removed by turning it anticlockwise. The rear of the lens is also covered with a cap that is removed in a similar way. To mount the lens, line up the red dots on the rear of the lens and front of the camera, and bring the two components together. Turn the lens clockwise until it clicks firmly into place.

To remove the lens, press the lens release button on the front of the camera and turn the lens anticlockwise (Diagram 6).

When the camera does not have a lens on it, always replace the body cap to stop dirt from entering. Avoid changing lenses in damp or dirty conditions. Never touch the mirror inside the camera. If the mirror gets dirty, use a blower brush to remove loose particles. If this is not enough, use a Prophot lens cloth to gently clean the mirror.

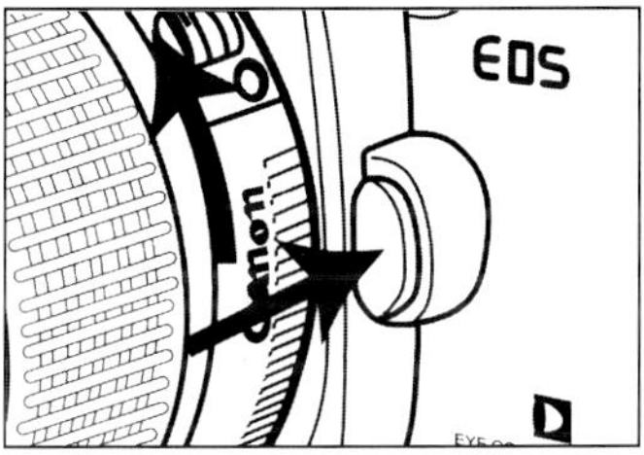

Diagram 6: *Press the lens release button and turn the lens anticlockwise to remove it.*

The neck strap

Your EOS 50/E – Elan II/E comes with a neck strap. This humble little accessory is often overlooked, but it can protect your camera from damage or loss. The strap is the most convenient way to carry your camera, and catches it if you should accidentally drop it.

Most people, when confronted by a strap and EOS camera, are puzzled as to how to put the two items together. It is not obvious how the strap attaches, but study diagram 7 and it will become clear. Make sure that you pull the ends of the strap after attaching it, to check that it is firmly in place. This is the only safe way to attach the strap, so don't try inventing your own way of doing it – you may put your camera at risk!

If you wish, you can replace the standard strap with an Op/tech camera strap that features a unique weight reduction system to make your camera feel much lighter and more comfortable to carry. Ask your photo dealer for details.

Now that you have attached the neck strap, always use it. If you drop your EOS, the strap will only be of use if it is around your neck!

Diagram 7: *This is the one and only way to attach the neck strap to your camera.*

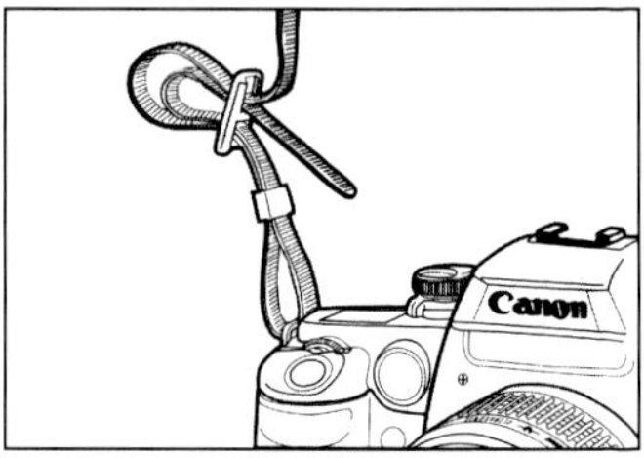

Loading a film

Your EOS 50/E – Elan II/E is of no use if it does not have a film in it. But don't load one immediately; take time to read this book and the instruction book to get to know the camera controls – leaving the film out gives you a chance to try out the camera without wasting frames.

When you feel ready to take some photographs, make sure that the main Command Dial is not set to Lock, then open the camera by pressing the camera back release button (Diagram 8) (get into the habit of looking through the little window in the back to make sure that there is not a film loaded before opening it). Now drop the film cassette bottom first into the space on the left of the camera (Diagram 8), and pull the film leader across to the orange mark (Diagram 9). Close the camera back. You will hear the sound of a motor as the camera winds the film onto the first frame. Look at the LCD panel; a film cassette symbol should have appeared, together with the number '1', telling you that the film has loaded correctly. If this symbol is flashing, the film has failed to load, open the camera back and check that the leader lines up with the orange mark before trying again.

After you have shot the last frame, the camera automatically rewinds the film into the cassette, ready to be removed for processing. When the film is fully rewound, the symbol in the LCD panel flashes, telling you that it is safe to open the camera back.

For more information on film rewind, turn to Chapter 11.

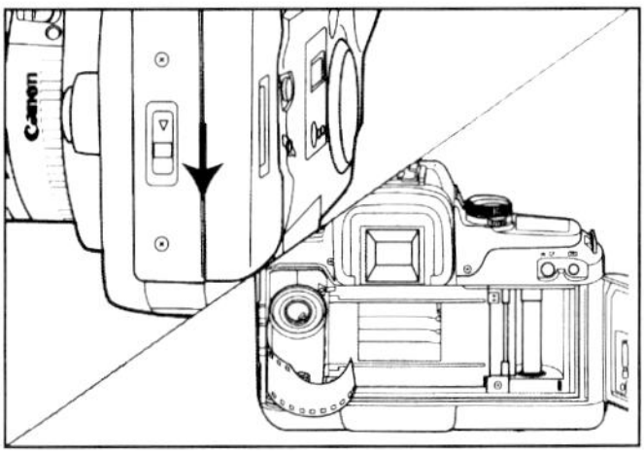

Diagram 8: *Open the camera back by releasing the catch on the end of the body. Insert the film bottom end first.*

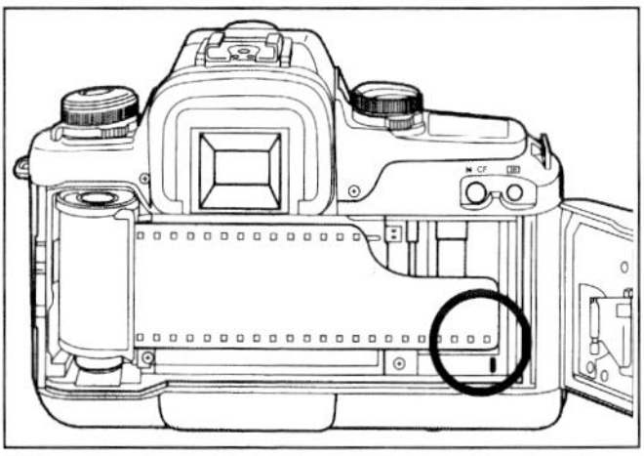

Diagram 9: *Pull the film leader across to the orange mark and then close the camera back.*

Film speed

The black and silver checks on a 35mm film cassette is a DX Code. This tells the camera what ISO setting to make, so there is normally no need to set the film speed yourself. The code also contains information on film length and type.

After the film has loaded, the ISO setting appears briefly in the LCD panel. Get into the habit of checking this each time that you load a film. Very occasionally, the camera fails to read the DX Code and therefore sets the wrong film speed.

If this happens, you must set the film speed yourself. You also have to do this if you are using a non-DX Coded film, or wish to alter the manufacturer's speed. To manually set the film speed, press the Function button on the back of the camera until 'ISO' appears in the LCD panel. Now turn the Electronic Input Dial until the desired film speed (between ISO 25 and 5000) shows in the panel. Wait six seconds or half press the shutter button to store the setting. This setting will be overridden when another film is loaded. You can use the Function button to display the film speed setting at any time.

Automatic film speed setting can be cancelled with Custom Function 3 – see Chapter 13.

Infrared film

Your camera instruction book states that infrared film cannot be used in the EOS 50/E – Elan II/E. This is because the camera's ultra-quiet film winding mechanism uses an infrared system to count the sprockets as the film travels through the counter. This can fog infrared film. However, the fogging is limited to the bottom 15% of the frame, and it may be much less with some films. Therefore, so long as you allow for this, you can use infrared film in your EOS 50/E – Elan II/E.

Chapter Four
Full Auto and PIC modes – taking your first pictures

Now that you have loaded your EOS 50/E – Elan II/E with a film and a battery, and attached the lens, you are ready to take photographs. If you have never used an EOS before, you may be bewildered by the camera controls, but you have no need to worry. Look at the main Command Dial and you will see a green square (Diagram 10). Switching the dial to this position sets Full Auto mode. This turns your EOS into a foolproof point-and-shoot camera – all you have to do is aim it in the right direction and press the shutter button; the camera does everything else for you.

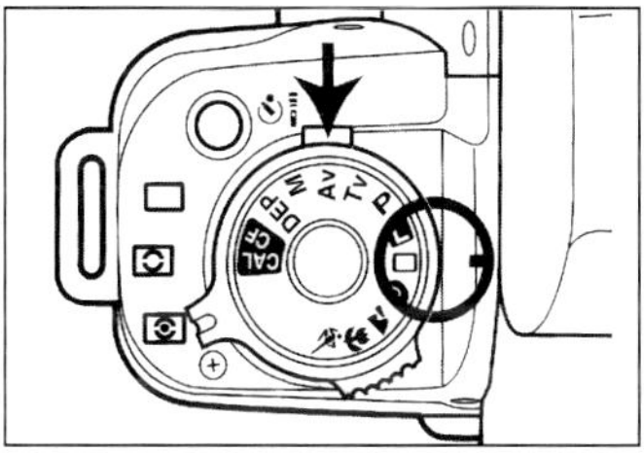

Diagram 10: *Turn the Main Command Dial to the green square to set Full Auto mode.*

Full Auto

Bring the camera to your eye and move around until the subject appears in the viewfinder. If necessary, adjust the lens zoom setting. Now half press the shutter button. The image snaps sharply into focus and you will hear a beep that tells you that the camera has successfully focused; a green circle appears in the viewfinder to confirm focus. Gently, but firmly, fully press the shutter button to take the photograph. Congratulations – you have shot your first EOS picture. Easy, wasn't it?

Full Auto mode looks after focusing, exposure metering, aperture and shutter speed. In low light, or outdoors in contrasty lighting, the built-in flash pops up when the camera senses it is required. Because Full Auto is designed to be foolproof, it is not possible to use functions such as Exposure Compensation and Auto Exposure Bracketing. Focusing is set to AI Focus, film advance to Single Frame and metering to Evaluative – it is not possible to alter any of these. Neither can you control when the flash fires.

Full Auto is so good that you will wonder why the camera needs other shooting modes! However, as you learn more about photography, you will start to want to take more control over the picture taking process, and you will find that Full Auto does not always give the result that you want.

But as you progress, don't forget about Full Auto mode – it is ideal for parties, family snapshots and other occasions when you don't want to worry about setting the camera. It is also useful when family and friends want to use your EOS.

PIC modes

Full Auto is good, but the settings that the camera makes in this mode have to be a compromise to ensure acceptable results with all subjects. That is why the EOS 50/E – Elan II/E also offers Program Image Control – commonly known as PIC modes.

PIC modes are similar to Full Auto in that the camera makes all the decisions for you, but the difference is that each PIC mode customises these settings to suit a particular subject.

Four PIC modes are available – Portrait, Landscape, Close-up and Sports. These are set by turning the main Command Dial to the relevant icon.

If you are an experienced photographer, you may be surprised by some of the settings that the camera chooses in PIC modes. This is because the modes are designed to be foolproof and extreme settings are avoided. These are explained under the heading for each PIC mode.

Portrait

Most of us take pictures of people – family, friends, or just interesting characters that we meet. Portrait mode, indicated by an icon of a woman's head (Diagram 11), helps to ensure that these pictures are flattering to the subject.

A wider lens aperture than normal is set to limit the depth-of-field and throw the background out-of-focus. This ensures that your subject stands out against their surroundings. For best results, use a lens setting of at least 80mm – 100mm, or 135mm is even better. Long focal lengths help to limit depth-of-field and put a comfortable distance between you and your subject.

Because people move about, Portrait mode sets film advance to Continuous. So if you keep your finger on the shutter button, the camera takes a series of pictures in quick succession – make sure that you have plenty of film! The built-in flash pops up and fires if it is required. Alternatively, you can use a Speedlite, this will fire for every shot.

Don't expect the camera to set the widest aperture, it is more likely to chose a mid-range setting to ensure that there is enough depth-of-field to allow for poor focusing. As you become more experienced you will want to change to Aperture Priority mode (see Chapter 5) for your portrait photography.

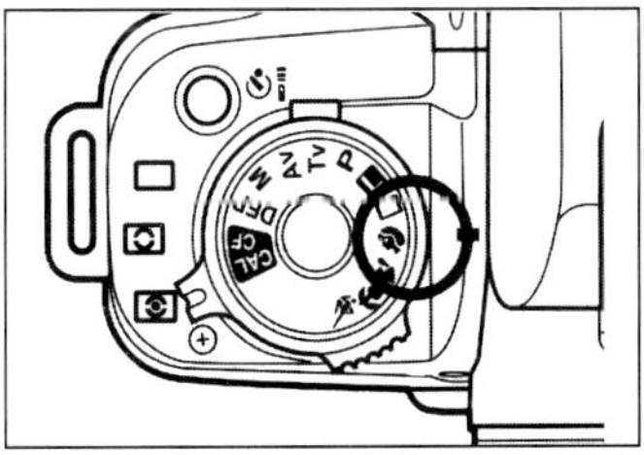

Diagram 11: *Turn the Main Command Dial to the icon of a woman's head to set Full Auto mode.*

Landscape

Landscapes are all around you – even if you live in a city you can find stunning vistas if you look. Landscape PIC mode is depicted by an icon of a mountain with a cloud (Diagram 12). Turn the main Command Dial to this setting to photograph distant scenes.

Most landscape pictures benefit from a small aperture to give maximum depth-of-field. However, this may lead to a long shutter speed being set, so Landscape PIC mode generally sets a smallish aperture that allows a fast enough shutter speed for hand-held photography. If you require the smallest aperture, set the camera to Aperture Priority mode (see Chapter 5) and be prepared to use a tripod or monopod.

Wide-angle lenses settings, such as 28mm or 35mm, are ideal for many landscapes because they increase depth-of-field and take in a large part of the scene. But don't forget that successful landscape shots can also be taken with telephoto lenses – don't be afraid to break the rules.

Because landscapes do not generally move, this PIC mode sets One Shot focusing and Single Shot frame advance with Evaluative metering. The built-in flash will not fire – no flashgun is powerful enough to illuminate a large scene! For this reason you should not have a Speedlite mounted for landscape pictures – it will fire if it is switched on and may cause the picture to be incorrectly exposed.

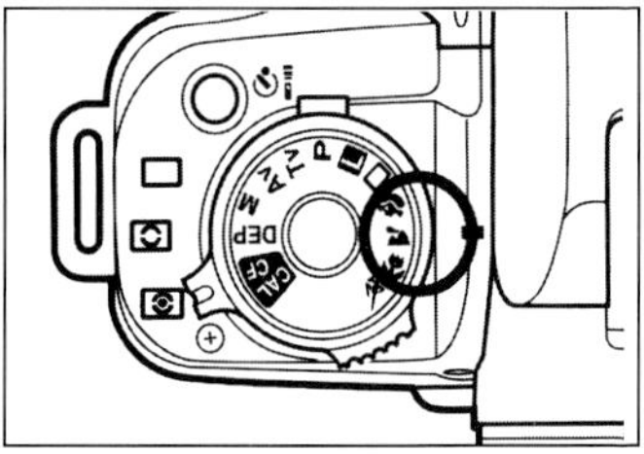

Diagram 12: *Turn the Main Command Dial to the icon of a mountain and a cloud to set Landscape mode.*

Sport

Sport PIC mode sets your EOS to shoot a variety of fast moving subjects, not just sports. Turn the main Command Dial to the icon of a runner (Diagram 13) and your EOS sets a faster shutter speed than normal to help freeze the movement of an action shot. AI Servo focusing (see Chapter 9) and Continuous film advance are also selected, together with Evaluative metering.

The built-in flash does not fire in Sport mode. As with Landscape mode, using a Speedlite may not give the results that you expect.

You will probably want to use a long focal length lens setting to enable you to get close to the action, and a high shutter speed also helps to avoid camera shake spoiling your pictures – long lenses not only magnify the image, they also magnify camera shake.

Sport mode may not set the fastest possible shutter speed, being a beginner's setting, it ensures that the aperture is small enough to give reasonable depth-of-field and therefore make sure that the subject is sharp. Use Shutter Priority mode (see Chapter 5) if you want to set the fastest possible shutter speed to freeze action.

Diagram 13: Turn the Main Command Dial to the icon of a runner to set Sport mode.

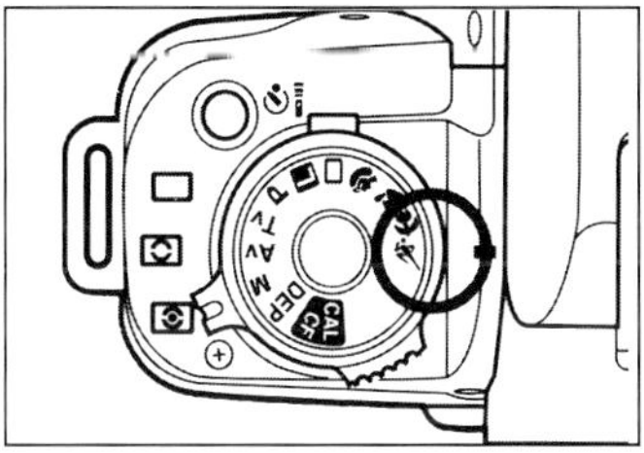

Close-up

Close-up photography opens up a whole new world. Everyday objects in your own backyard become exotic subjects to point your EOS at. Many EF lenses focus close enough for low-power close-up work – look for a yellow flower on the lens barrel.

For straightforward close-up photography with one of these lenses, turn the main Command Dial to the icon of a flower (Diagram 14). This mode chooses a smallish aperture to increase depth-of-field, which decreases as you get closer to a subject. But very small apertures are not set in close-up mode because they may lead to shutter speeds too long for hand-held photography.

Most close-up subjects are photographed in the centre of the frame, so Close-up mode sets the camera to Partial metering. This takes an exposure reading from the centre of the frame and ignores the surroundings. Focusing is set to One Shot, and film advance to Single Frame.

The built-in flash fires if it is required. If you are using a Speedlite, this will always fire.

To get in closer to your subject, you will need a special EF Macro lens (see Chapter 19), extension tube or a supplementary close-up lens (see Chapter 20).

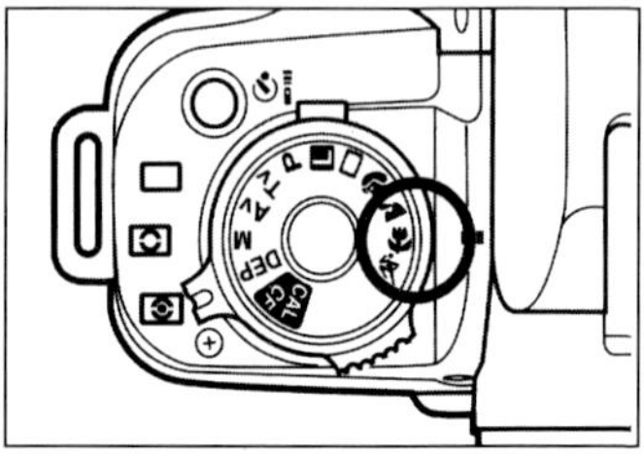

Diagram 14: *Turn the Main Command Dial to the icon of a flower to set Close-up mode.*

Chapter Five
Beyond the basics – Creative Zone modes

Now that you have mastered Full Auto and PIC modes you will want to take more control over your photography. Look at the main Command Dial; on the opposite side of the Lock position to the PIC modes are the Creative Zone settings. These give you the control that you want, while still letting you make use of the camera's sophisticated metering systems.

The main difference between Full Auto and PIC modes and the Creative Zone settings is that the latter give you access to Exposure Compensation (Chapter 8), Auto Exposure Bracketing (Chapter 8), AE Lock (Chapter 7) and Multiple Exposures (Chapter 12). You can also choose the metering mode (Chapter 7), focus mode (Chapter 9) and film winding mode (Chapter 11).

Let's look at each Creative Zone mode in detail.

Program

In Program mode – the 'P' setting on the main Command Dial (Diagram 15) – your EOS 50/E – Elan II/E selects both an aperture and a shutter speed to give a correct exposure for the conditions.

You may think that this sounds the same as Full Auto mode, and in some ways it is. The exposure settings that the camera makes are identical, but the difference is that you can alter these settings by using other camera functions such as Exposure Compensation.

Unlike Full Auto mode, the built-in flash does not automatically fire in Program mode. If you wish to use the flash, you must activate it manually; it then behaves the same way as when Full Auto is set.

Program mode is ideal for a range of photographic situations where you do not wish to set a specific aperture or shutter speed. In fact, it is a good mode to leave your camera in for taking most of your pictures. When you use Program mode, keep an eye on the viewfinder display so that you can check that the aperture and shutter speed are suitable for the effect that you desire.

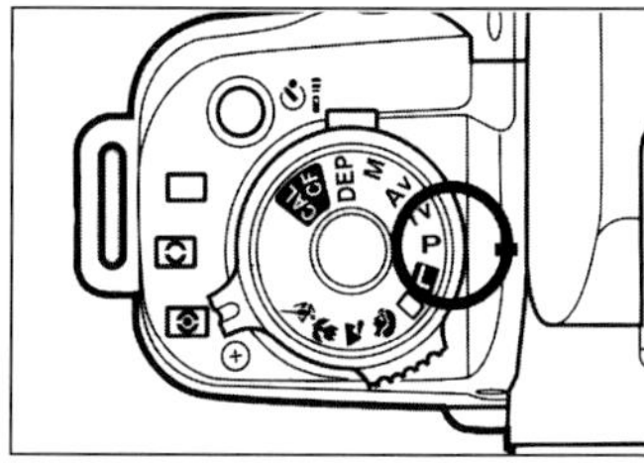

Diagram 15: Turn the Main Command Dial to 'P' to set Program mode.

Program Shift

The most powerful way that you can alter the exposure settings made by the camera in Program mode is to use Program shift.

This under-used feature allows you to alter the aperture and shutter speed set by the camera, while still retaining a correct exposure. It relies on the fact that increasing the shutter speed by one stop halves the amount of light reaching the film, and opening the aperture by the same amount doubles the amount of light. So as the shutter speed increases, the aperture opens to compensate. In other words, you shift the settings.

Program Shift provides a useful way for beginners to start controlling shutter speed and aperture without switching to Aperture Priority or Shutter Priority modes. It can also be used by more experienced photographers in rapidly changing lighting conditions when there is not enough time to switch to another mode.

Program Shift is very simple to use. After you half press the shutter button to focus and take an exposure reading, the camera displays the chosen aperture and shutter speed in the viewfinder. If you then turn the Electronic Input Dial, say, two clicks clockwise (when looking from the back of the camera), the shutter speed increases by one stop. At the same time, the aperture opens by one stop to ensure that the exposure remains constant. For instance, if the camera sets 1/125 seconds at f8, turning the Electronic Input Dial two clicks clockwise shifts the settings to 1/250 at f5.6. This gives exactly the same exposure. Turning the Electronic Input Dial the other way decreases the shutter speed and sets a smaller aperture.

It is not possible to set a shutter speed or aperture that will not give a correct exposure – if you turn the Electronic Input Dial beyond the widest aperture, Program Shift stops operating. This means you cannot set an incorrect exposure.

Remember that if you choose a long shutter speed, you may need to use a tripod or monopod to avoid camera shake spoiling your photograph.

Do not use Program Shift if you wish to take a number of photographs at the same aperture and shutter speed – the settings are lost after you have pressed the shutter button. Program Shift does not operate during flash photography, with neither the built-in flash or a Speedlite.

Shutter Priority

Turn the main Command Dial to 'Tv' (Diagram 16) to set Shutter Priority mode (Tv stands for Time Value – a little used photographic expression). In this mode you choose the shutter speed by turning the Electronic Input Dial until the desired setting appears in the viewfinder and LCD panel. The camera then sets an aperture that will ensure a correct exposure.

However, the camera may not be able to give a correct exposure. For instance, in dim conditions, you are unlikely to be able to set a shutter speed of, say, 1/4000 sec – even the widest aperture setting will not allow enough light to reach the film. Or in very bright conditions, the camera may not be able to set a small enough aperture if you have chosen a longer shutter speed, say 1/4 second. If the light is too bright or too dark for a correct exposure, the viewfinder display will flash. You must turn the Electronic Input Dial to alter the shutter speed until the flashing stops. If you do not do this, you will still be able to fire the shutter, but the photograph will not be correctly exposed. Light conditions change, so keep an eye on the display to make sure that it is not flashing. If the light drops, you may have to set a longer shutter speed.

Use Shutter Priority mode when shutter speed is important. For instance, during action photography when a fast speed will help to freeze action. Or when you are using a telephoto lens and a shutter speed of at least 1/focal length is needed to minimise camera shake during hand-held photography. For instance, if you are using a 200mm lens, the shutter speed should be 1/200 second or faster.

This mode is also useful when you wish to set a long shutter speed to blur movement – for instance, when photographing running water.

Remember to keep an eye on the aperture setting – too wide an aperture limits depth-of-field, whereas a small aperture makes everything in the frame appear sharp. It is up to you to decide which effect you require.

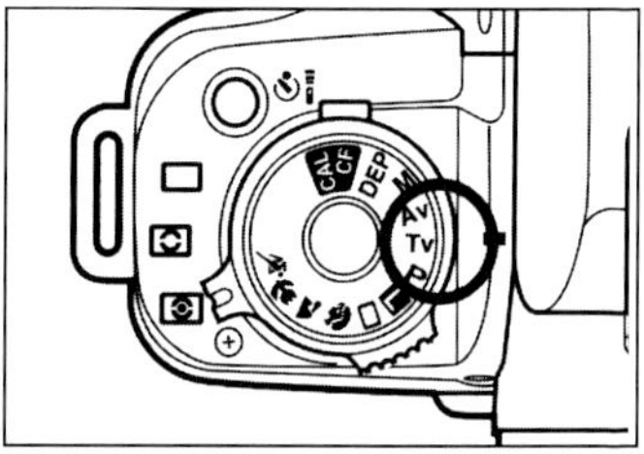

Diagram 16: *Turn the Main Command Dial to 'Tv' to set Shutter Priority mode.*

Aperture Priority

Aperture Priority mode is the opposite of Shutter Priority – you select the aperture and the camera sets a corresponding shutter speed. Switch your EOS 50/E – Elan II/E to Aperture Priority mode by turning the main Command Dial to 'Av' (Aperture Value) (Diagram 17).

The aperture is set by turning the Electronic Input Dial until the desired value appears in the viewfinder and LCD panel. If the viewfinder and LCD panel flash, the camera is unable to set a shutter speed that will give a correct exposure. When this happens you must alter the aperture by turning the Electronic Input Dial until the flashing stops. If you do not do this, the shutter will still fire, but the photograph will be incorrectly exposed.

In Aperture Priority mode, it is important to keep an eye on the shutter speed. If you set a small aperture, such as f5.6, the camera may set a long shutter speed to ensure that enough light reaches the film. If this happens, you must mount the camera on a tripod, monopod or other firm surface to avoid camera shake spoiling the photograph. Alternatively, set a wider aperture to bring the shutter speed up to hand-holding levels.

Use Aperture Priority mode when you want to limit depth-of-field. For instance, setting a wide aperture, such as f4, limits the depth-of-field and throws backgrounds, or foregrounds, out-of-focus. This is a useful technique for portrait photography because it gives you a sharp face against a blurred background. A short telephoto lens, such as 100mm, further limits depth-of-field and so is ideal for portrait work.

Aperture Priority mode is also useful when you require maximum depth-of-field to ensure that as much of the subject as possible appears sharp in the picture – landscape photography, for example. Also, it is the ideal mode for close-up and macro photography. As you get closer to a subject, depth-of-field becomes more limited, so you need to set a small aperture to give as much sharpness as possible.

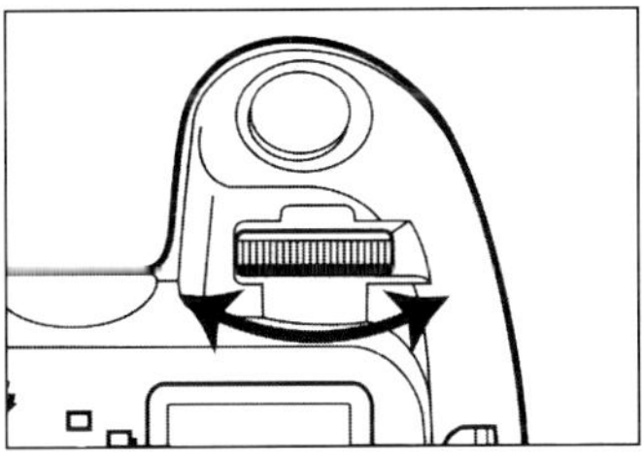

Diagram 17: *Turn the Main Command Dial to 'Av' to set Aperture Priority mode.*

Manual

You may be surprised that your EOS 50/E – Elan II/E has a Manual mode. After all, it gives such good results when you leave it to get on with the job, why bother setting the aperture and shutter speed yourself? To be honest, there are only a few occasions when you need to set Manual, but it is a mode worth knowing about.

When you turn the main Command Dial to 'M' (Diagram 18), your EOS 50/E – Elan II/E relinquishes control of shutter speed and aperture, leaving you to make both settings. But don't worry, the camera exposure meter remains active to guide you if you wish.

The shutter speed is adjusted by turning the Electronic Input Dial. The aperture is set by rotating the Quick Control Dial on the back of the camera (make sure that it is switched on).

When you look into the viewfinder in Manual mode and half press the shutter button to focus, the display shows a linear scale with an arrow. When this arrow is set to '0', the exposure, according to the camera, is correct. You must adjust the aperture and shutter speed to achieve this. If the arrow blinks at -2 or +2 stops, the picture will be under or overexposed by more than two stops. Exposure Compensation is not possible in Manual mode.

The best way to use Manual mode is to first decide what is more important – shutter speed or aperture. For instance if you decide that you require maximum depth-of-field, set a small aperture such as f22. Now half press the shutter button and look at the viewfinder display. If necessary, adjust the shutter speed until the arrow under the linear scale is set to '0'.

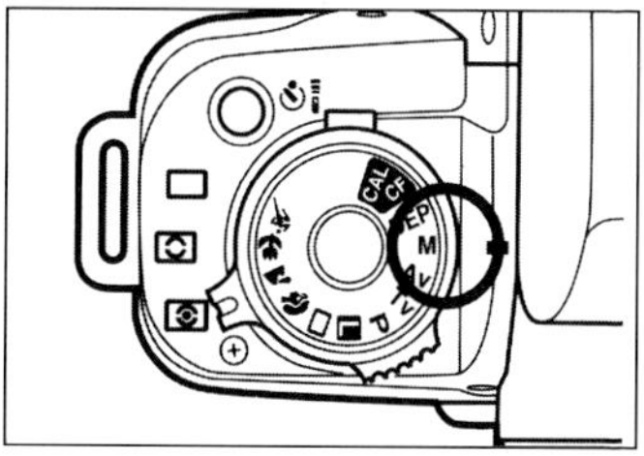

Diagram 18: *Turn the Main Command Dial to 'M' to set Manual mode.*

Here are some situations when manual mode is useful:

Learning about photography

Your EOS 50/E – Elan II/E gives incredibly accurate exposures in Full Auto, PIC and Creative Zone modes, the latter allowing you to override the settings. But taking total control of exposure from time to time is an excellent way to learn more about photography. It also slows down the picture-taking process, forcing you to spend more time thinking about each shot, rather than clicking madly away. Then when you return to using the camera in another mode, you will have a better idea of what the camera is doing and why it makes the settings it does. Don't forget that you can make use of the camera's built-in exposure meter in Manual mode.

Using a separate light meter

The Evaluative and Partial metering systems of your EOS 50/E – Elan II/E are so accurate that there is really no need to use a hand-held light meter. However, you may prefer to use one for some of your pictures, in which case you must put your camera into Manual.

Taking a reading from a grey card

Your EOS 50/E – Elan II/E metering system assumes that the subject you are photographing is a mid-tone – an average of dark and light tones – and will set an exposure that will make the photograph appear the same brightness. A typical mid-tone is a white person's skin or a grass lawn.

A grey card is a board with a mid-tone grey surface. This can be positioned so that it receives the same light as the subject, and an exposure reading taken from it, making sure that it fills the frame in the viewfinder. By putting the camera into Manual, you can hold this reading when you remove the grey card and recompose the subject.

Grey cards are most commonly used when photographing paintings and other flat artwork.

Using a single exposure setting

There are situations when the light is constantly changing, but you want to leave the shutter speed and aperture unaltered. In an automatic setting, the camera will alter the settings to suit the changing light.

For instance, at a pop concert there are often flashing coloured lights in the background, while the performers are lit by a more constant white light. By putting your EOS 50/E – Elan II/E in Manual, and taking a partial meter reading from a performer's face, you can ensure that all the frames will be exposed the same and not affected by the background lighting.

Using non-dedicated flashguns

When using non-dedicated flashguns and studio flash units, your EOS 50/E – Elan II/E must be set to Manual. See Chapter 16 to find out more.

Macro flash photography

When taking macro or close-up photographs with a Speedlite flashgun, you should set the camera to Manual, flash control will still be automatic.

Bulb setting

Normally, the longest shutter speed possible with your EOS 50/E – Elan II/E is 30 seconds. However, when your EOS 50/E – Elan II/E is in Manual mode , you have access to a unique setting – Bulb.

To set Bulb, first make sure that the camera is in Manual mode and then turn the Electronic Input Dial towards the longest shutter speeds; when you get to 30 seconds, keep going – the LCD panel will display 'buLb'.

When your EOS 50/E – Elan II/E is set to Bulb, the shutter remains open as long as the shutter button is kept fully depressed. That means that there is no limit to the length of your exposures.

Bulb is used in very low light, when even 30 seconds is not long enough for a correct exposure, although it can also be used for setting shorter exposures. The camera must be mounted on a sturdy tripod to ensure that it does not move during the exposure. Ideally, you should use a remote release (see Chapter 20) to activate the shutter – it is hard to keep your finder pressed down on the shutter button without moving the camera. You need to use a stop-watch or count 'elephants' to time Bulb exposures.

In case you are wondering, the term bulb comes from the days when photographers used pneumatic releases to fire their cameras. These consisted of long tubes with rubber bulbs on the end.

Chapter Six
Depth-of-field

Depth-of-field is something that you must learn to control in order to take better photographs. Before looking at how your EOS 50/E – Elan II/E lets you do this, let's find out a little about depth-of-field.

What is depth-of-field?

Depth-of-field is the distance between the nearest and farthest points in a photograph that appear acceptably sharp. It is not, as many people think, the amount of the picture that is in focus. A lens only focuses on one point at a time – anything closer or farther from the lens is out-of-focus but may appear to be sharp.

Depth-of-field depends partly on aperture. When you set a wide lens aperture, such as f4, depth-of-field is minimal, and only the area that the lens is focused on appears sharp. However, by stopping down to a small aperture, such as f22, much more of the scene appears sharp, even though it is still technically out-of-focus.

Focal length has an effect on depth-of-field. As the focal length of a lens increases, depth-of-field decreases. Therefore, a wide-angle lens is able to give more depth-of-field than a long focal length lens.

Another factor influencing depth-of-field is lens-to-subject distance. As the lens gets closer to the subject, depth-of-field decreases. This becomes particularly apparent during macro photography when the lens may be just a few centimetres from the subject. Therefore, you must set the smallest possible aperture to ensure that the subject appears acceptably sharp.

Focusing and depth-of-field

Some people think that setting a small aperture means that they do not have to worry too much about focusing. But depth-of-field does not increase the area that is in focus, only the amount of acceptable sharpness. You should always take care to focus on the most important part of your subject.

If you are photographing a scene that you wish to be sharp from foreground to background, use a wide-angle lens, select Aperture Priority mode, set a small aperture and focus one-third of the way into the picture. This will ensure maximum depth-of-field. Remember that a small aperture may lead to a long shutter speed, so be ready to use a tripod or monopod.

Depth-of-field mode

Although Aperture Priority mode is suitable for controlling depth-of-field, the EOS 50/E – Elan II/E boasts a Depth mode. To select this, turn the main Command Dial to the 'DEP' setting (Diagram 19).

Depth mode allows you to select the nearest and farthest points that you want to appear sharp in a scene. The EOS 50/E – Elan II/E then selects an aperture that will give sufficient depth-of-field, as well as focusing at the optimum distance. A shutter speed is set that will ensure a correct exposure with the selected aperture.

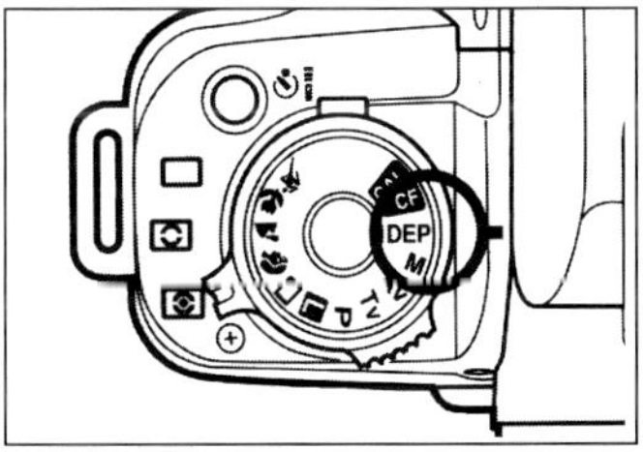

Diagram 19: *Turn the Main Command Dial to 'DEP' to set Depth-of-field mode.*

How to use Depth mode

Depth mode works with all types of focus point selection – manual, automatic and Eye-control. When automatic point selection is set, the camera uses only the centre focus point. When Manual or Eye-control selection is used, you can specify any of the points. However, only one focus point is used, and that may as well be the centre one – there is no advantage in using one of the outside focus points with Depth mode. The lens must be set to autofocus.

Look through the viewfinder at your subject and decide the nearest area that you wish to appear sharp. Aim the selected focus point at this and press the shutter button. 'dEP 1' will appear in the viewfinder and LCD panel (Diagram 20), and the green in-focus mark lights. Remove your finger from the shutter button.

Now aim the focus point at the farthest point that you wish to appear sharp. Press the shutter button again. 'dEP 2' will appear in the viewfinder and LCD panel (Diagram 21) and as before, the green in-focus mark lights. Remove your finger from the shutter button.

Recompose the viewfinder image and press the shutter button to take the photograph. The LCD panel will display the set aperture and shutter speed (Diagram 22). Remember that Depth mode does not necessarily give you maximum depth-of-field; just enough to cover the areas that you have selected. If you change your mind halfway through the process, you can cancel Depth mode by turning the main Command Dial to another position.

Depth mode is not only for ensuring sufficient depth-of-field, it can also be used to limit it. Setting the two Depth mode points on the same part of the subject causes the camera to select the maximum aperture and throws the background and foreground out-of-focus. Of course, you can achieve the same effect more easily in Aperture Priority mode!

Diagrams 20, 21 and 22:

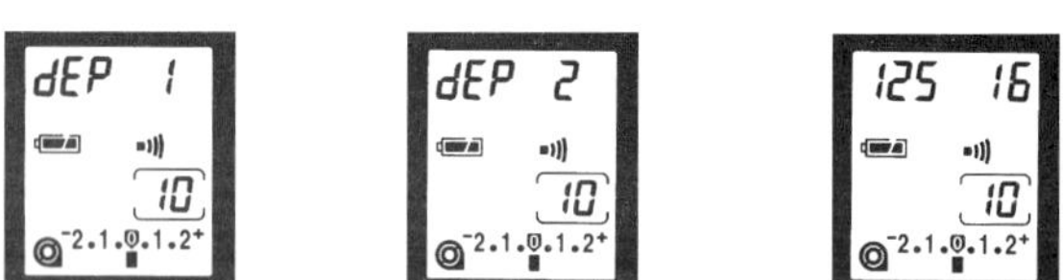

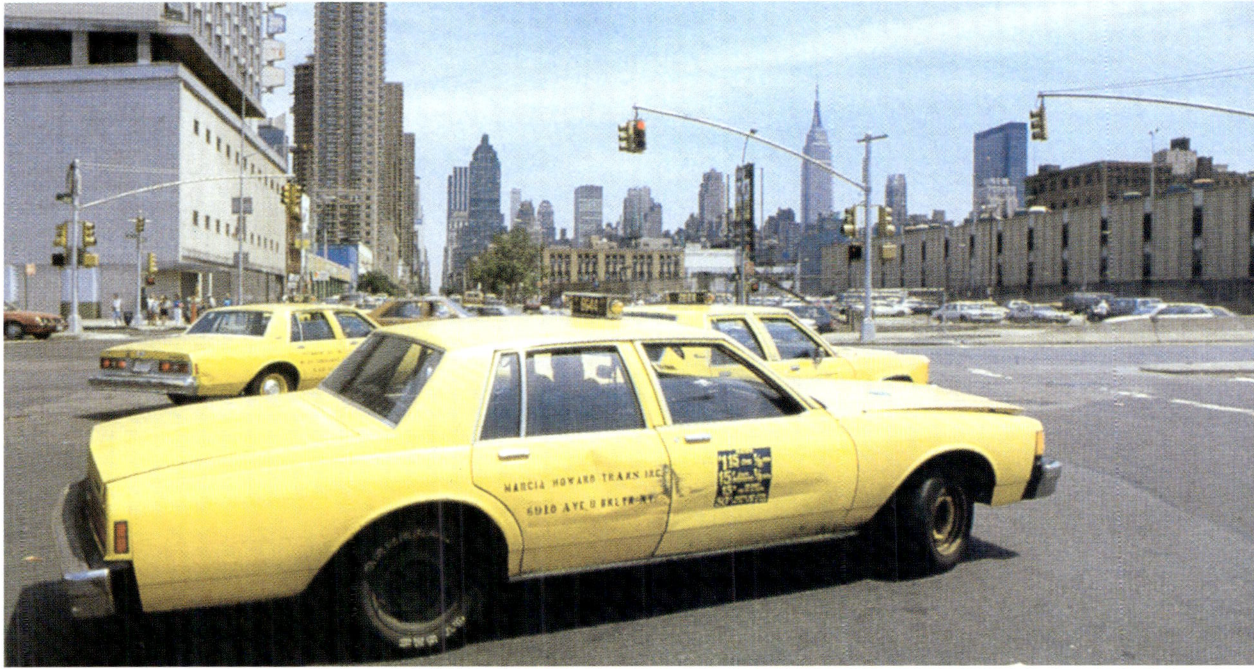

Full Auto mode is a useful mode to leave your EOS50/E - Elan II/E in for snatch shots. A 28mm lens setting has captured this typical New York City street scene.

Photograph: Philip Raby

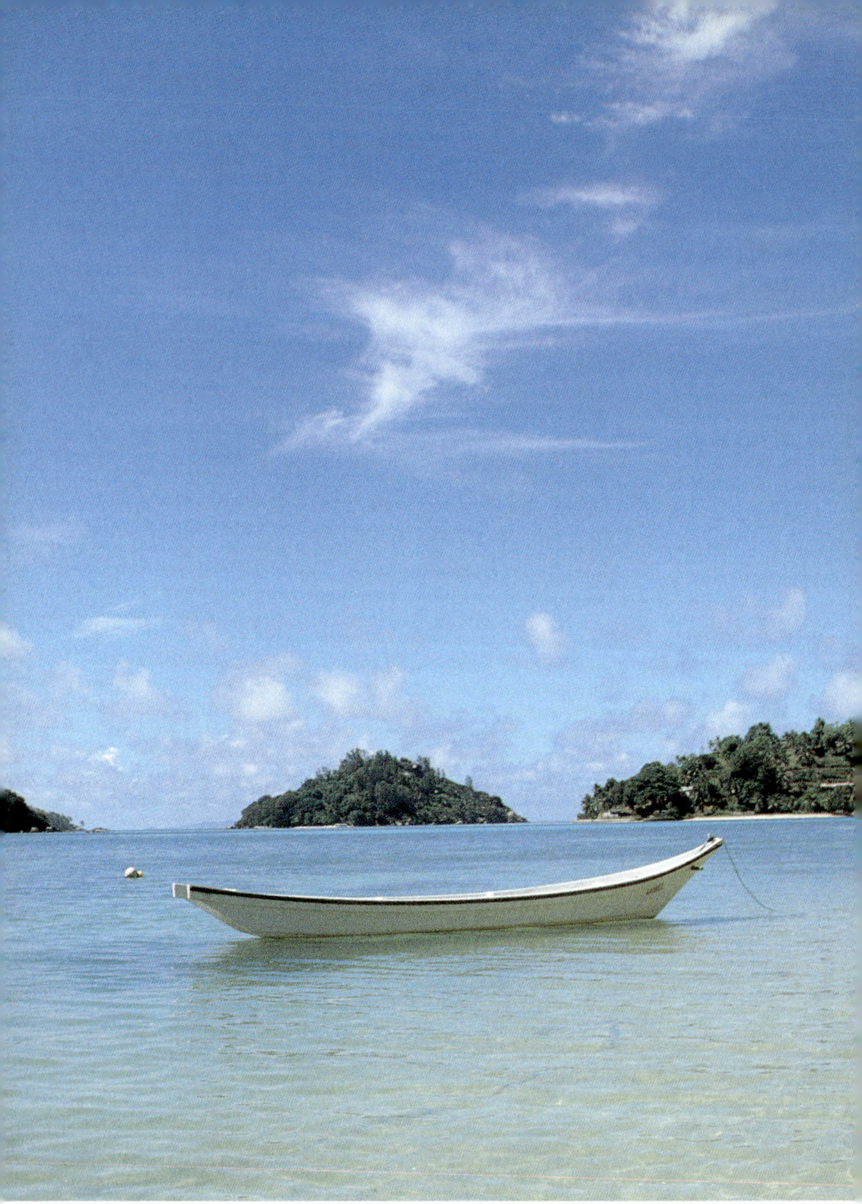

Landscape mode is suitable for any views, including seascapes. This tranquil scene was shot with Landscape mode and a wide-angle lens setting.

Photograph: Philip Raby

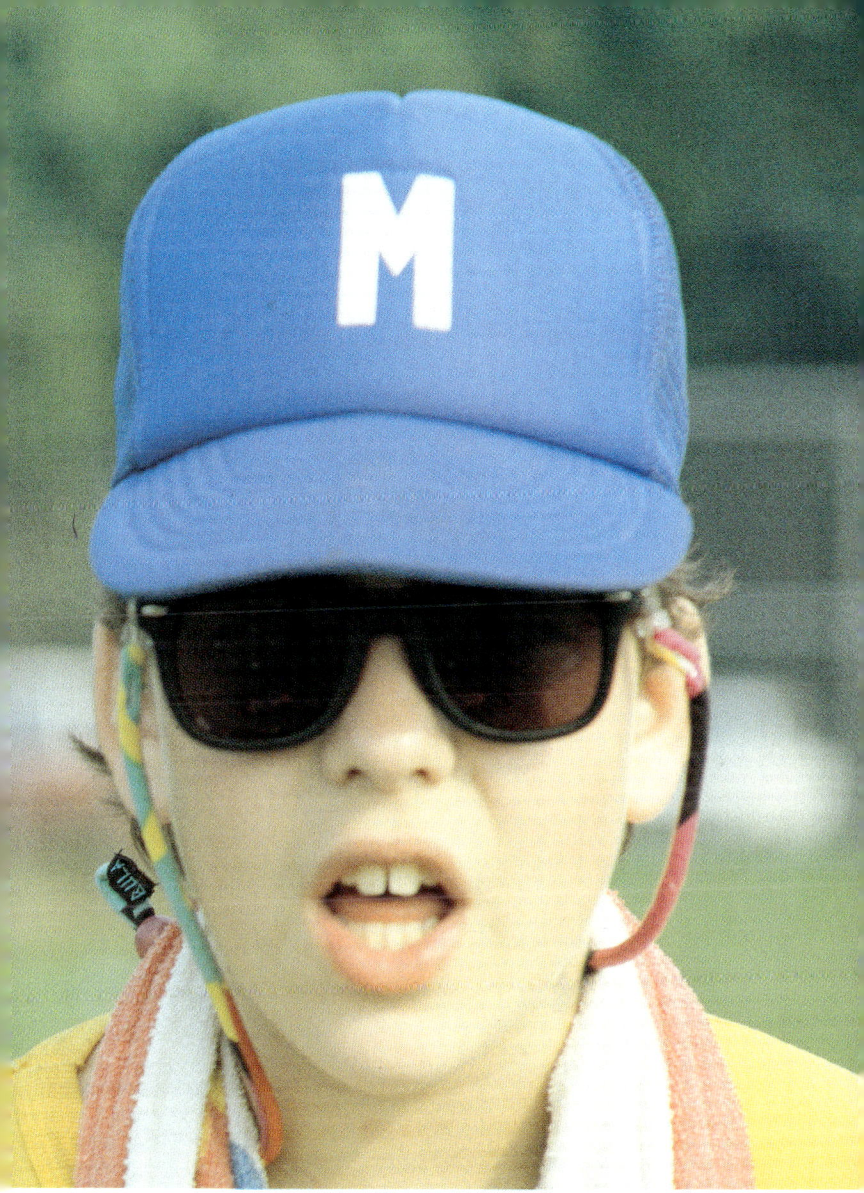

Portrait mode sets a wide aperture to throw backgrounds out-of-focus and so make the subject stand out.

Photograph: Philip Raby

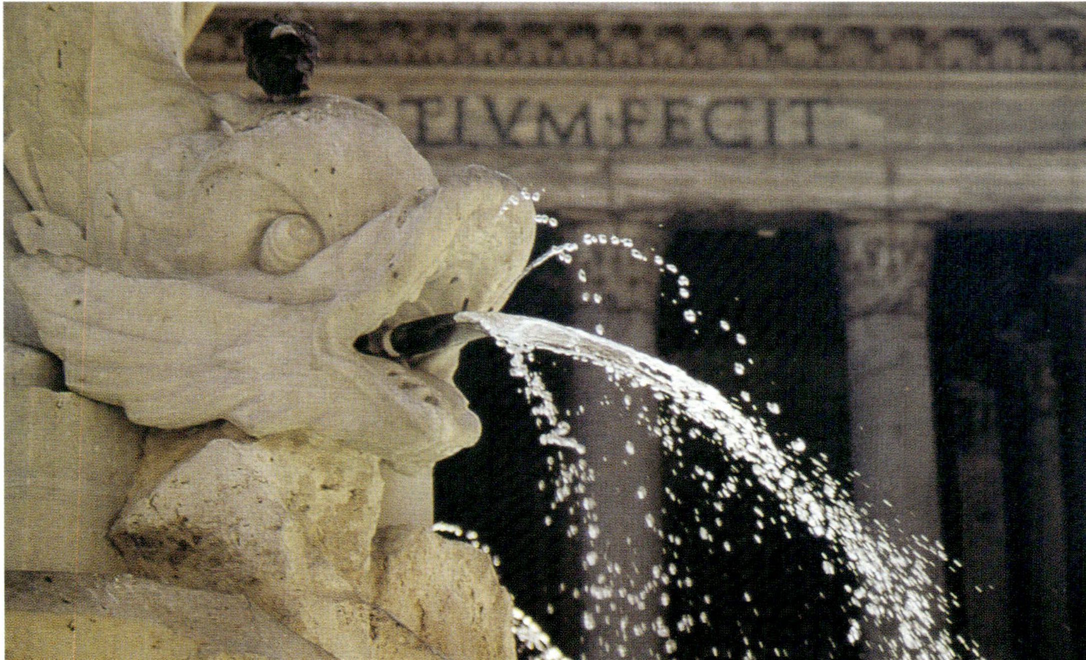

Sports mode is not just for sports, it can be used for any fast-moving subject. Here, a high shutter speed has frozen the movement of the drops of water coming from the statue's mouth.

Photograph: Philip Raby

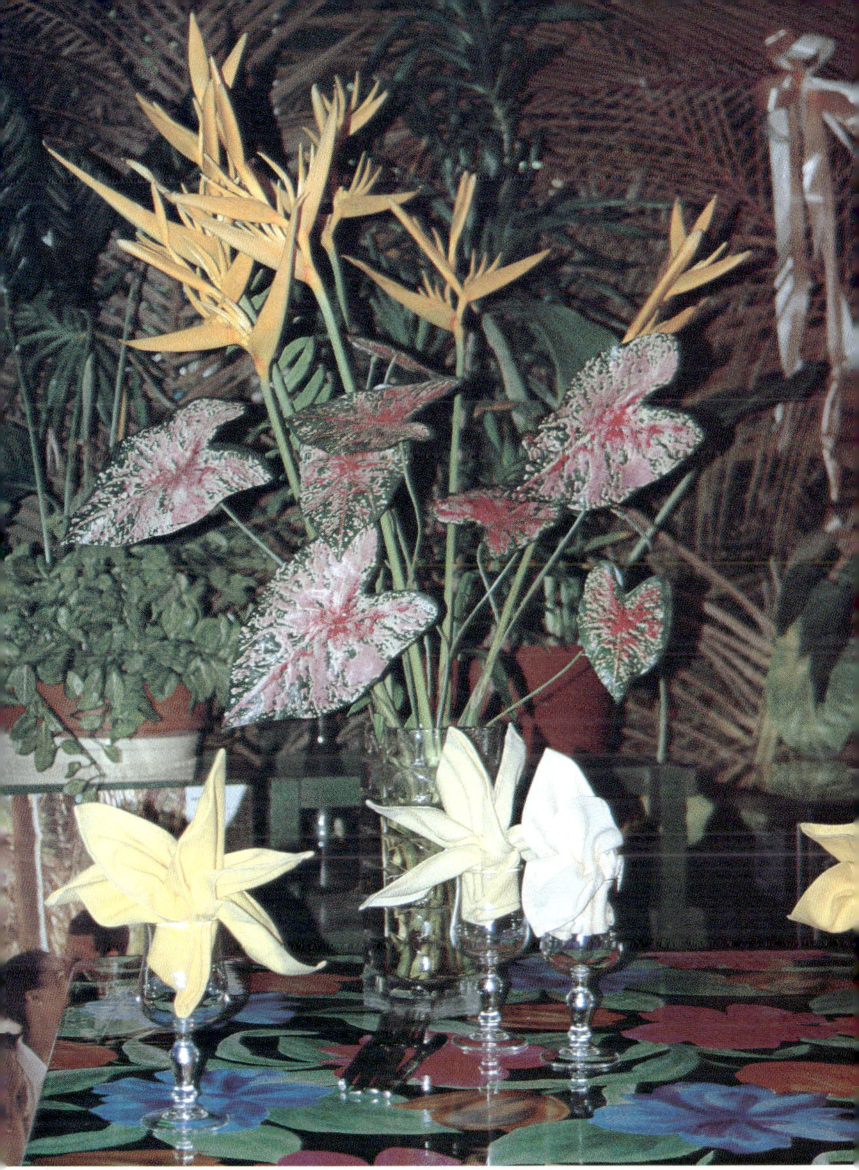

Close-up mode is not designed for true macro photography. However, it is ideal for close-up snapshots. This flower arrangement was photographed between courses at a Seychelles restaurant. Illumination is from the built-in flash.

Photograph: Philip Raby

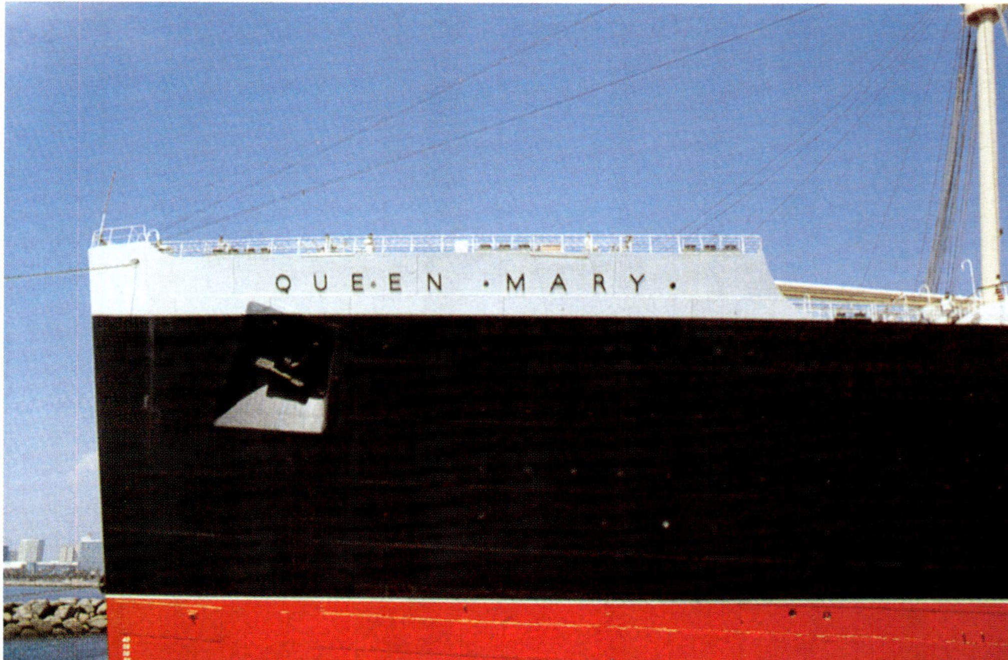

Set Program mode if you do not need to control shutter speed or aperture. This close-up of the Queen Mary in Los Angeles is a graphic study of lines and colour.

Photograph: Philip Raby

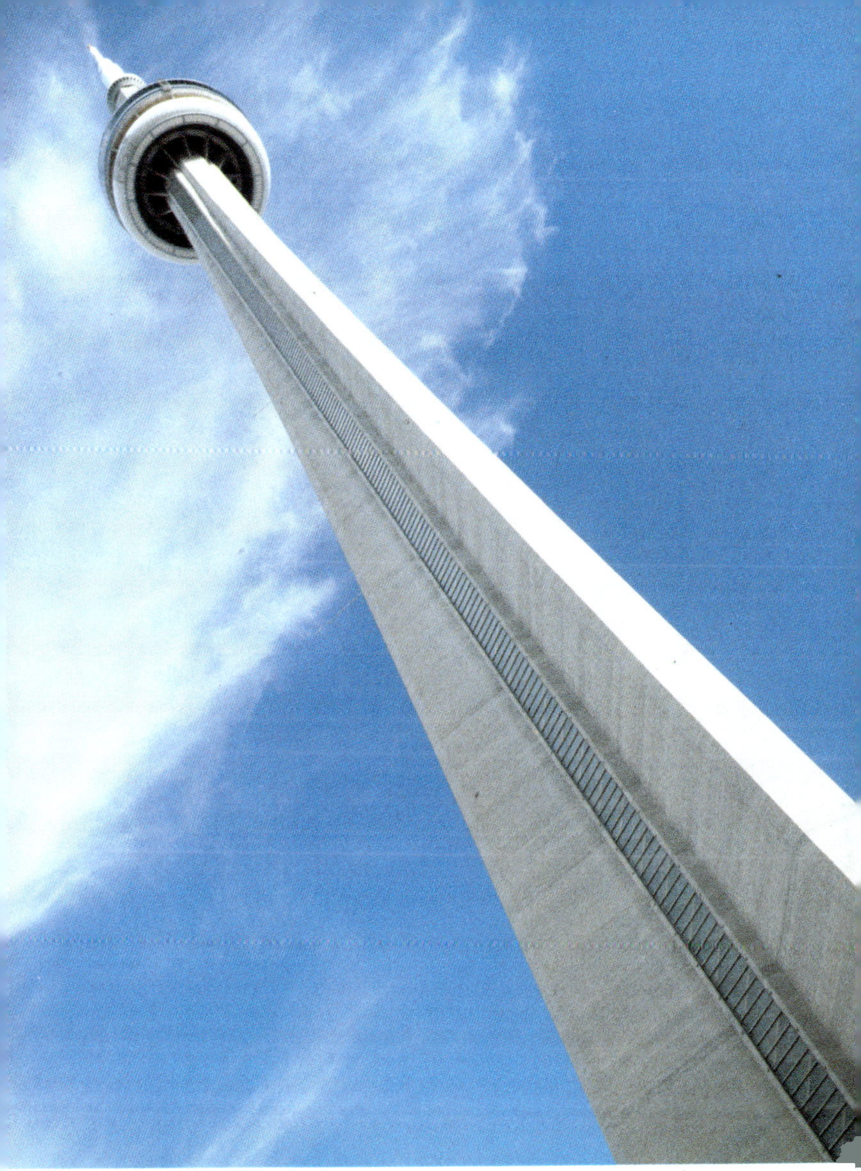

Choose Aperture Priority mode if you want to control aperture and depth-of-field. A small aperture and wide-angle lens setting has ensured that the world's tallest building - the CN Tower in Toronto - is sharp from bottom to top.

Photograph: Philip Raby

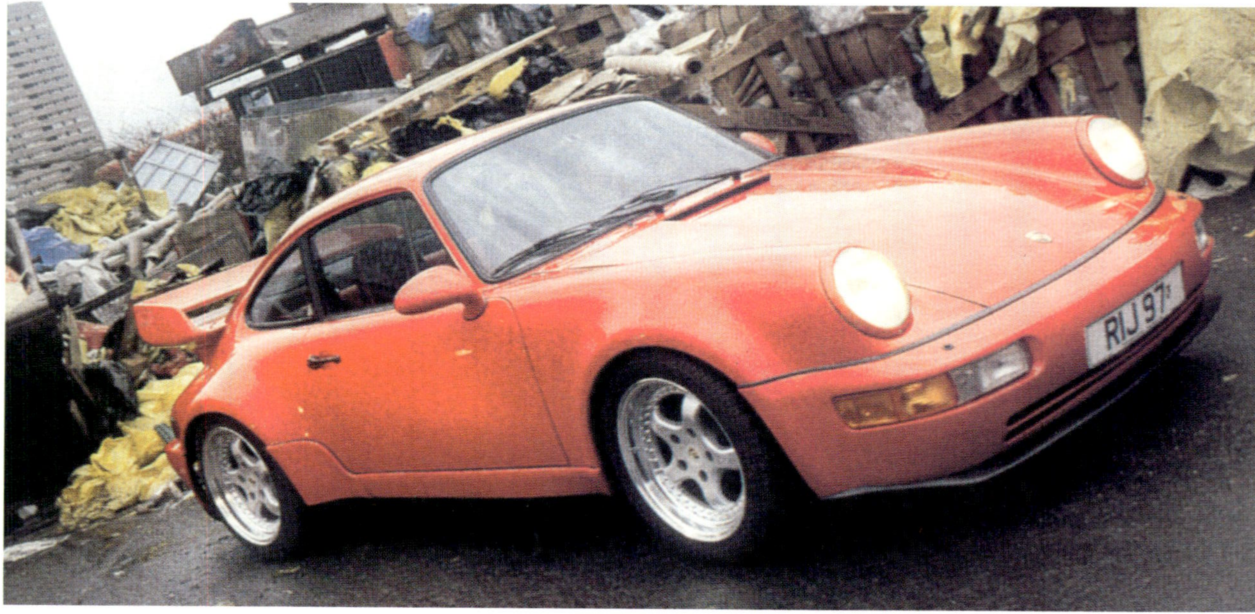

Don't give up if the weather is bad. This customised Porsche 911 was photographed on a very dull winter day. Another car was positioned to the left of the camera so that its headlamps illuminated the subject. A Speedlite 540EZ was mounted on camera in A-TTL mode to add more light. To add interest, the Porsche's headlamps were also switched on.

Photograph: Philip Raby

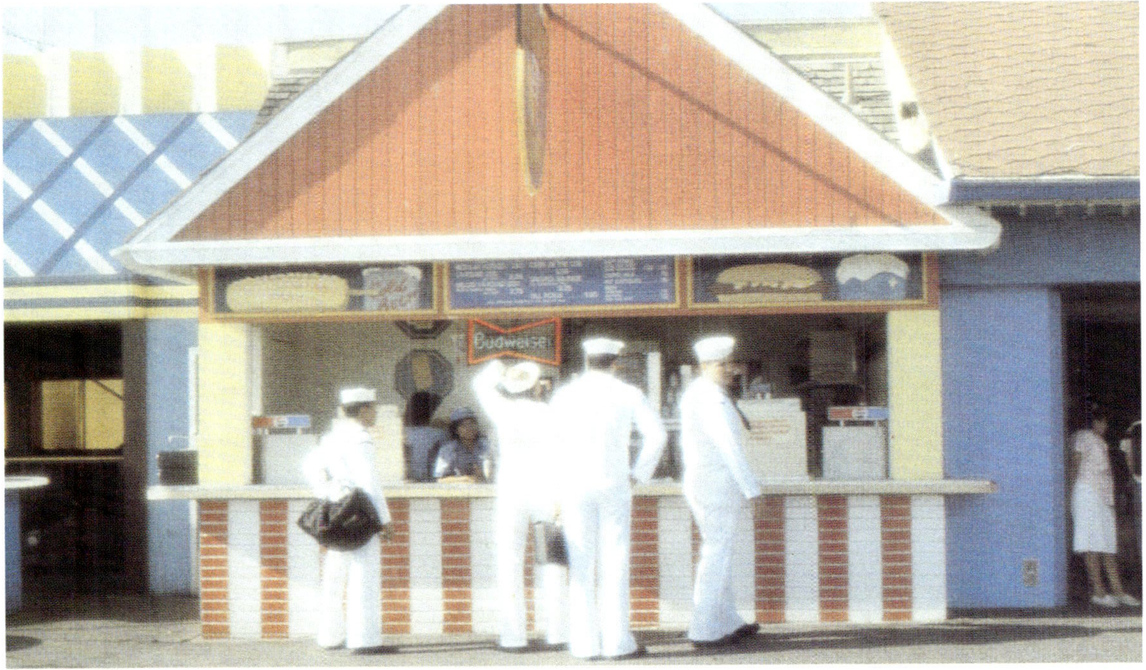

This shot of sailors at a Santa Cruz burger bar is typical old-time America. The dated look was achieved by using a soft-focus filter and slight overexposure to give a pastel effect.

Photograph: Philip Raby

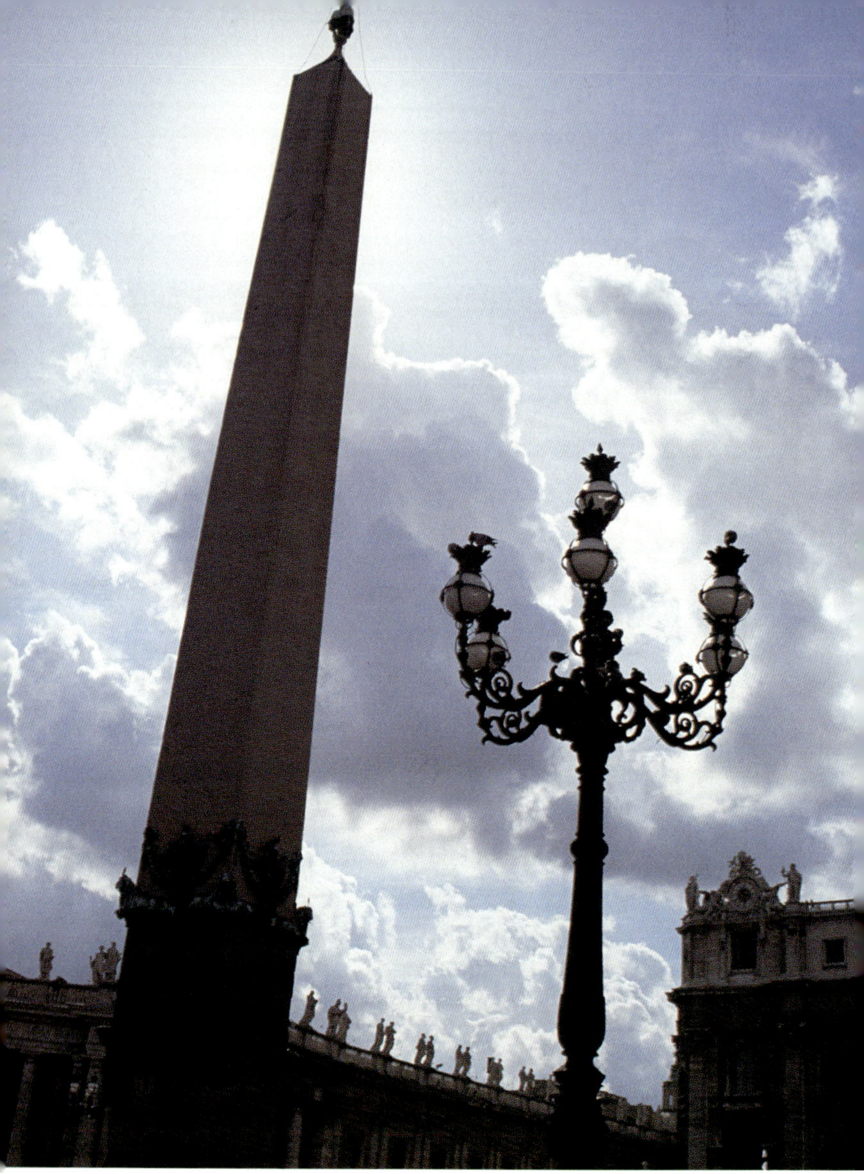

The Evaluative metering of EOS 50/E - Elan II/E is remarkably good at coping with difficult lighting conditions. This scene of St Peter's Square, Rome, was shot in Program mode with no exposure compensation. The result is a dramatic silhouette.

Photograph: Philip Raby

If, after selecting the two points, the aperture value flashes in the viewfinder, the amount of depth-of-field required is not possible – the camera will give as much as it can. You may be able to get around the problem by moving away from the subject – depth-of-field increases with distance. Alternatively, use a wider focal length lens setting – wide-angle lenses give more depth-of-field than telephoto ones.

If the shutter speed flashes at 30 seconds and the maximum aperture flashes, there is not enough light to take the photograph in Depth mode. Increase the lighting or load a faster speed film. Conversely, if the shutter speed flashes at 1/4000 second together with the minimum aperture, there is too much light. Load a slower speed film or attach a neutral density filter to the lens (a neutral density filter reduces the amount of light that reaches the film without affecting it in any other way).

In Depth mode, your EOS 50/E – Elan II/E may set a long shutter speed to compensate for a small aperture. Keep an eye on the viewfinder display and if the shutter speed becomes too long for hand-held photography mount the camera on a tripod or monopod.

Do not try and use flash in Depth mode, it will not work and the camera will revert to Program mode.

Depth-of-field Preview

When you look through the viewfinder of your EOS 50/E – Elan II/E, you will not see the effect of the aperture on depth-of-field. This is because the aperture diaphragm is always wide open until the moment that you press the shutter button, when it closes down the pre-selected amount. If it did not do this, the viewfinder image would be too dark to see clearly at small apertures.

However, your EOS 50/E – Elan II/E allows you to stop down the aperture, prior to taking the photograph, to enable you to see how much of the subject will appear sharp in the photograph.

If you have an EOS 50E – Elan IIE, you can do this when Eye-control focus is activated. Look into the viewfinder and you will see a diamond shaped marker in the top left corner. Glance at this while keeping the shutter button partly depressed and the aperture will stop down to the chosen setting. You have six seconds after focusing to do this. (Custom Function 11 must be set to '0' for Eye-control depth-of-field preview to operate.) Eye-control depth-of-field preview does not operate in conjunction with AI Servo focusing.

Both the EOS 50 – Elan II and EOS 50E – Elan IIE offer depth-of-field preview by setting Custom Function 4 to '2'. This turns the AE Lock button into a depth-of-field preview button. Press it and the aperture immediately closes down.

You will find that at very small apertures the viewfinder image becomes very dark during depth-of-field preview. This is because less light is reaching the focusing screen. However, it is normally bright enough for you to assess the amount of sharpness.

You do not have to let the aperture open up before taking the photograph. However, when using a Speedlite 380EX, the aperture will automatically open right up before the preflash fires.

Depth-of-field the lazy way

If all this sounds like too much bother, many photographers get excellent results by using a simple rule-of-thumb. Set a small aperture for maximum depth-of-field, and a wide aperture to limit depth-of-field. Not very scientific, but it works!

Chapter Seven

Metering modes

For a good photograph, the film in your camera must receive just the right amount of light. Too little and the photograph will be dark (underexposed), too much and it will be too bright (overexposed). The amount of light that reaches the camera depends on two things – the shutter that controls the amount of time that the film is exposed to light, and the aperture that determines the brightness of the light which reaches the film.

Back in the old days, before electronic cameras, photographers had to either guess the aperture and shutter speed, using their experience and guides supplied with films (sunny weather: 125th at f11; cloudy weather: 60th at f4), or, for more accurate results, use a hand-held exposure meter.

But your EOS 50/E – Elan II/E uses state-of-the-art electronics to measure the amount of light passing through the lens and reaching the film. This is called Through-The-Lens, or TTL, metering and means that poorly exposed photographs are almost a thing of the past. Even the most inexperienced photographer can achieve superb results at the push of a button.

The EOS 50/E – Elan II/E offers three types of exposure metering – Evaluative, Centre-weighted Average, and Partial. These are set by the metering mode lever – the peripheral thumb control on the main Control Dial.

Evaluative

This is the mode that you should use for most of your photographs. It is also the mode that is chosen by the camera in Full Auto and PIC modes (except Close-up that uses Partial metering). To set Evaluative metering, turn the metering mode lever anticlockwise as far as it will go.

Evaluative metering divides the subject area into six zones, and a meter reading is taken from each zone (Diagram 23). The camera's microprocessor analyses these readings and compares them with sample readings stored in memory. It is able to assess whether the subject is backlit or particularly bright or dark, and sets the shutter speed and aperture accordingly. What's more, it assumes that the area that you have focused on is to be correctly exposed, and biases the exposure to the active focus point.

Evaluative metering copes with most lighting conditions, and you will find very few occasions when you cannot trust it to get on with the job.

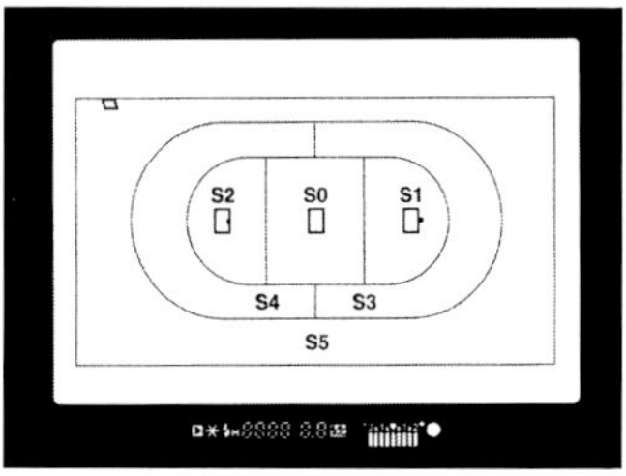

Diagram 23: *Evaluative metering divides the subject area into six zones.*

Centre-weighted Average ▭

Before the days of Evaluative metering, Centre-weighted Average was the metering system used in most Canon cameras. It takes a reading from the whole of the scene, but with a bias to the central area, the assumption being that the main part of the subject will be in the centre of the picture.

Centre-weighted Average gives good results with most subjects, but may be confused with backlit, bright, or dark subjects, as well as off-centre ones.

To set Centre-weighted Average, turn the metering mode lever clockwise as far as it will go.

The reason that Canon has included Centre-weighted Average on the EOS 50/E – Elan II/E is because some photographers have grown up with the system and know what sort of results to expect. If this applies to you, by all means use Centre-weighted Average, but do give Evaluative metering a try – it really is better!

Partial metering

As its name suggests, Partial metering takes an exposure reading from just a small part of the subject area. Normally, the reading is taken from the centre 9.5% of the viewfinder image – around the centre focus point (Diagram 24).

Partial metering is used when the subject that you are photographing is surrounded by an expanse of bright or dark areas. Although Evaluative metering can cope with most situations, it may be confused by a dominant or dark background and expose for that rather than the subject. Partial metering allows you to take a reading just from the part of the subject that you wish to reproduce as a mid-tone. It is very useful for portraits.

Partial metering is set in Close-up PIC mode because the main subject is usually in the centre of the frame during macro photography.

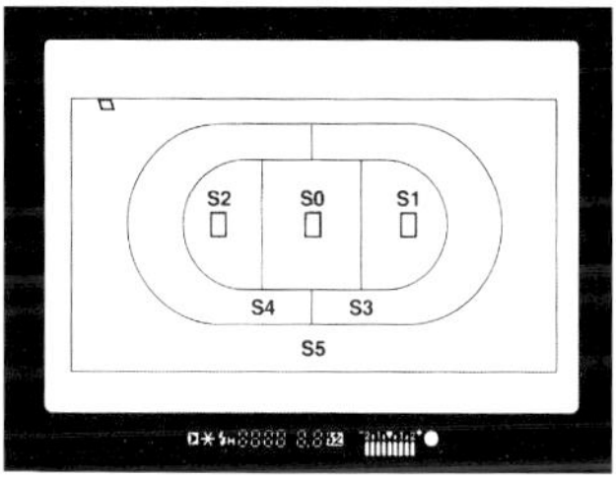

Diagram 24: *Partial metering takes a reading from just the centre of the frame.*

How to use Partial metering

Set Partial metering by turning the metering mode lever to the centre position. To take a partial meter reading, aim the camera so that the part of the subject you wish to reproduce as a mid-tone appears in the centre of the viewfinder. Now half press the shutter button to activate the meter. If you wish to recompose the picture before firing the shutter, press the AE Lock button to hold the exposure reading.

Setting Custom Function 8 to '1' alters Partial metering so that the reading is taken from the active focus point. This reduces the need to use AE Lock when taking a reading from an off-centre subject.

Stop-down metering

Stop-down metering is not mentioned in the camera instruction book and most photographers are unlikely to need it. It is only required when you have a non-dedicated lens or accessory attached to your EOS 50/E – Elan II/E. This may be a mirror lens, slide copier, Canon Auto Bellows, or a Canon FD mount lens attached with an adaptor.

A dedicated lens is able to communicate with your camera through a series of gold-plated contacts and tell it what its maximum aperture is. A non-dedicated accessory is unable to do this, so the camera has to meter the light in a different way to ensure a correct exposure. This system is called stop-down metering.

Your EOS 50/E – Elan II/E automatically switches to stop-down metering mode when a non-dedicated lens or accessory is attached in Aperture Priority mode. The camera displays an aperture of f0.0 and will set a suitable shutter speed. If you are using a Speedlite flashgun, set the camera to Manual and choose a shutter speed no faster than 1/125 second, the flash will adjust to give a correct exposure.

AE Lock

AE Lock (also known as Exposure Lock) allows you to take a light reading from one part of a scene, and hold it while you recompose the photograph. Although it can be used with any metering mode, AE Lock is normally used in conjunction with Partial metering.

To use AE Lock, point the camera at the area that you wish to be exposed as a mid-tone. Now press the AE Lock button on the back of the camera (Diagram 25). The exposure settings will lock, even if you take your finger off the button. To cancel the setting, press the button again to take another reading, switch off the camera, or wait six seconds for the viewfinder display to cancel.

Use Partial metering and AE Lock in situations when the subject is surrounded by a light or dark background. For instance, when photographing a white person against a dark wall, Evaluative metering will try to expose for the wall and give an overexposed face. Therefore, take a Partial reading from the face, and hold it with AE Lock while you recompose the picture. A white person's skin is a mid-tone, so the camera will ensure that is correctly exposed.

__Diagram 25:__ Press this AE Lock button to hold a meter reading.

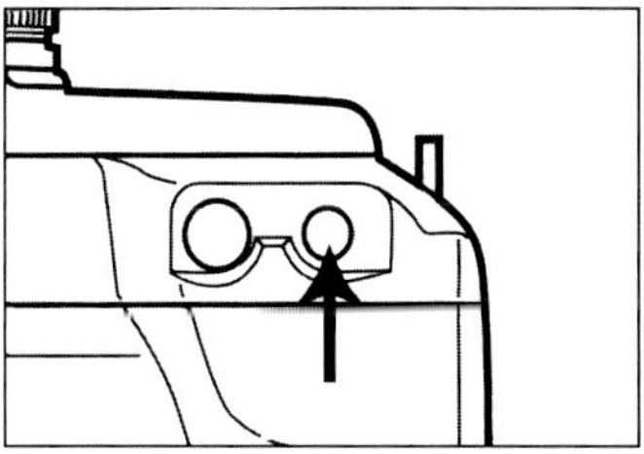

Chapter Eight
Exposure Compensation

Whichever metering system you choose, you can be certain that it will give superb results in most situations. However, just occasionally, you need to override the camera's selected shutter speed and aperture. You can do this by setting Manual mode (see Chapter 5), but it can be easier to use Exposure Compensation in Creative Zones. This allows you to alter the setting made by the camera by up to ±2 stops in 1/2 stop intervals.

The camera does this by altering the shutter speed, aperture, or both. In Shutter Priority mode, the aperture changes, in Aperture Priority mode, the shutter speed alters, and in Program mode, either or both settings change.

Exposure Compensation is not possible when the camera is set to Manual.

How to set Exposure Compensation

Before setting Exposure Compensation, you must focus and take an exposure reading in the normal way by half pressing the shutter button.

Within four seconds of doing this, turn the Quick Control Dial (Diagram 27) (make sure that it is turned on) until the desired amount of compensation appears on the bar graphs in the LCD panel and viewfinder display (Diagram 28). Moving the arrow below the scale to the left decreases the exposure in 1/2 stop increments down to -2 stops. Moving the arrow to the right increases the exposure up to +2 stops in the same increments.

If you want to use the same amount of Exposure Compensation for a number of photographs, turn off the Quick Control Dial by setting its switch to '0'. This will ensure that Exposure Compensation is not accidentally altered.

Remember that Exposure Compensation remains set until you cancel it by turning the Quick Control Dial until the bar graphs in the LCD panel and viewfinder are set to zero.

Always check that the arrows are at zero to make sure that Exposure Compensation is not set when it is not required.

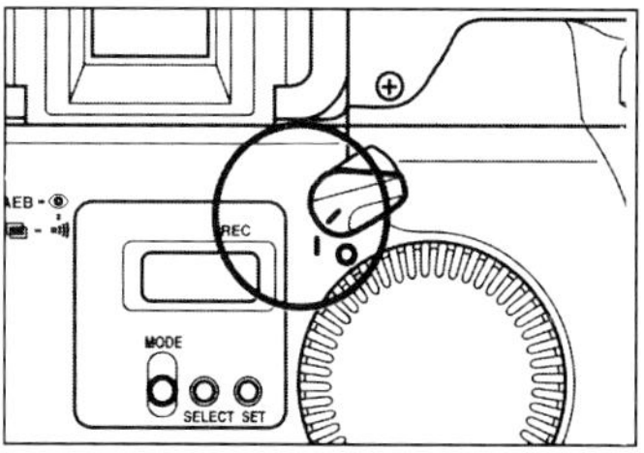

Diagram 26: *Turn on the Quick Control Dial by turning the switch to 'I'.*

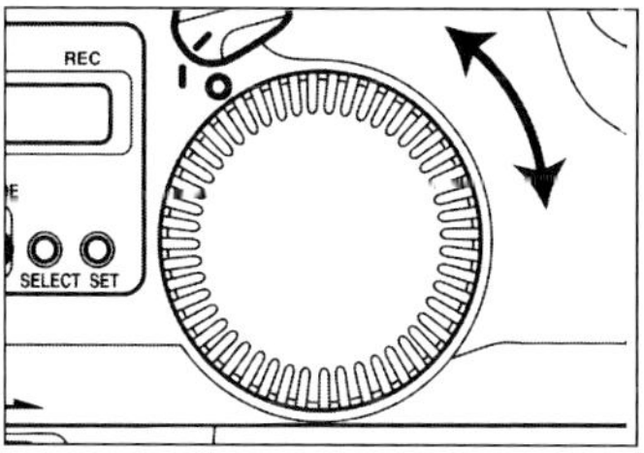

Diagram 27:
Turn the Quick Control Dial to set the required amount of Exposure Compensation.

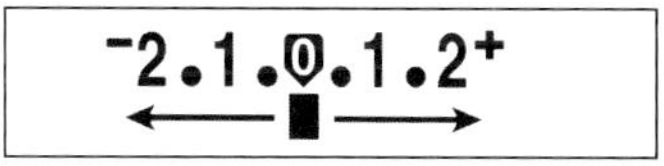

Diagram 28: *Turning the Quick Control moves the pointer under the bar graph to the left or right.*

When to use Exposure Compensation

As you develop as a photographer you will learn to recognise times when you need to alter the exposure set by the camera. Here are some common situations:

In the snow

You know that snow is white. However, the light meter in your EOS 50/E – Elan II/E does not – it assumes that any subject is a mid-tone. Therefore, it reproduces snow, or any other white or light subject, as a murky grey. So, if your subject is predominantly white, set exposure compensation to +1.5 stops to ensure a pure white result.

In the dark

The opposite of white objects is a pile of coal, or any other dark or black subject. The camera again assumes that the subject is a mid-tone and exposes accordingly, giving a grey result. To ensure black tones in the photograph, underexpose the film by about -1.5 stops.

Increasing colour saturation

The ISO film speed rating suggested by the film manufacturer is the one to use in most situations. However, colour slide film occasionally benefits from slight underexposure. This increases the saturation of bright, deep colours. Until you have learnt when to use this technique, take two shots – one with Exposure Compensation and a second picture without. Colour print (negative) film does not benefit from underexposure in this way.

Soft focus

A range of lenses and accessories is available to degrade the sharp image formed by your camera. The reason for doing this is to create a soft focus image for portraits and dreamy effects.

Many soft images are enhanced by slight overexposure to wash out the highlights and give a light, dreamy atmosphere.

Auto Exposure Compensation (AEB)

If you don't know whether to under or overexpose a shot, or indeed whether compensation is required, don't worry. You can set your EOS 50/E – Elan II/E to take three frames – one with minus compensation, one without compensation, and a third overexposed by a chosen amount. When you get the film back from the processors, you can choose which frame is the best. If you think that shooting three frames is wasteful, it is much better than taking one unsuccessful picture – especially if the shot is unrepeatable.

This feature is called Auto Exposure Compensation (AEB) and is used mainly with colour slide film – negative film has a wider exposure latitude and slight changes to exposure are less noticeable.

How to set AEB

To set AEB, press the Function button on the back of the camera until 'AEB' appears in the LCD panel (Diagram 29). Now turn the Electronic Input Dial until the desired bracketing amount appears in the LCD panel. The amount of compensation can be set in 1/2 stop intervals to two stops. For instance, if AEB is set to 1.0, three pictures will be taken: one at the correct exposure determined by the camera, one under exposed by one stop and a third overexposed by one stop.

To take the pictures, press the shutter button all the way in the usual way. If continuous film winding is set, you can take all three shots one after the other simply by holding down the shutter button.

AEB is not automatically cancelled after taking a photograph, so you can take a series of pictures using the facility. After you have finished using AEB, cancel it by pressing the Function button until 'AEB' appears in the LCD panel and then turn the Electronic Input Dial to return the bracketing amount to zero.

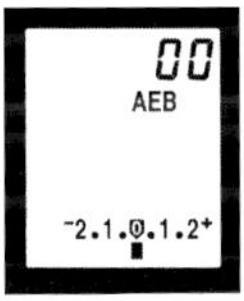

Diagram 29: *'AEB' appears in the LCD panel when Auto Exposure Bracketing is being set.*

Combining AEB with Exposure Compensation

Because AEB is a form of exposure compensation, you may be surprised to know that it can be used in conjunction with the camera's Exposure Compensation feature. You should do this when you know which direction the compensation should be set, but are unsure how much to set.

For example, white subjects should be overexposed, so it would be a waste of a frame to set AEB to give an underexposed shot. The answer is to set the required AEB setting and then set Exposure Compensation to twice that amount. For instance, set AEB to +0.5 stops and Exposure Compensation to +1 stop. The camera will then give three images, overexposed by +0.5, +1 and +1.5 stops

Chapter Nine
More about focusing

Using your camera in Full Auto and PIC modes will have shown you just how fast and accurate the EOS autofocus system is. There is a lot more to discover about focusing and how to use it to its best advantage. First of all, let's look at the different focus modes you can choose in Creative Zone settings. These settings are made with the second Command Dial (Diagram 30).

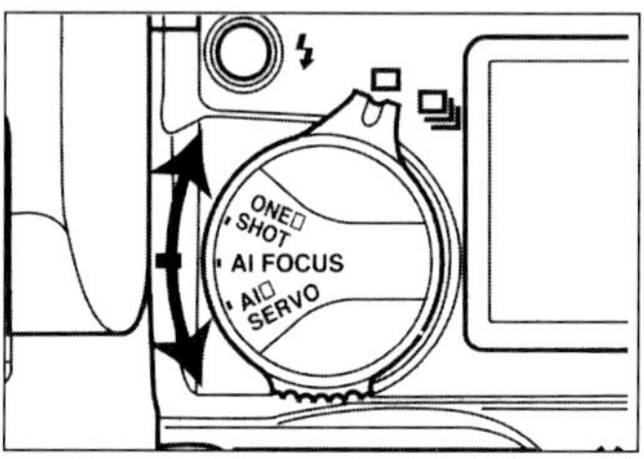

Diagram 30: *The focus mode is set with the second Command Dial.*

One Shot

One Shot is the focusing mode to use for photographs of static subjects and portraits. Set it by turning the second Command Dial fully anti-clockwise.

When you half press the shutter button, the lens focuses. The focus setting is then locked as long as you keep your finger on the button. This feature is known as Focus Lock – you can recompose the photograph knowing that the focus setting you have made will not change.

When the lens focuses in One Shot mode, a green in-focus symbol appears in the viewfinder and the camera beeps (if the sound is turned on – see Chapter 2) to confirm correct focus. If the camera is unable to focus, you will be unable to take a photograp).

AI Servo

Turning the second Command Dial fully clockwise sets focus to AI Servo mode. This is the mode to use for action photography. Instead of the focus locking, like in One Shot mode, it continually refocuses as the lens-to-subject distance changes. This means that you can track a moving subject.

Be careful in AI Servo mode – the shutter fires even if the subject is not in focus, so make sure that you only press the shutter button when you know that focus is correct.

Predictive Focusing

When a subject is moving towards you at high speed, it can travel a considerable distance in the short time between you pressing the shutter button and the shutter actually firing. Although we are only talking milliseconds here, it can be enough to throw a fast-moving subject out-of-focus. To compensate, the EOS 50/E – Elan II/E has Predictive Focusing in AI Servo mode. As you track the subject the camera uses the information gained by the lens continually refocusing to calculate the speed that the subject is travelling. It can then predict the lens-to-subject distance at the moment of exposure.

Predictive Focusing is activated automatically in AI Servo mode, you will be unaware of it happening.

AI Focus

If you are unsure whether your subject is going to be moving or static, set the second Command Dial to the centre position. This sets AI Focus. In this mode, the camera assesses subject movement and automatically sets either One Shot or AI Servo focusing. However, you will find that a subject needs to be moving quite fast for the camera to choose AI Servo.

Manual Focus

There are times when you need to focus manually. To set manual focus, slide the switch on the lens to 'M' (Diagram 31). This switches off autofocus completely. The letters 'M.F' appear in the LCD panel to warn you.

To focus manually, turn the focus ring on the lens (or

the lens barrel if the lens does not have a ring) until the viewfinder image appears sharp (Diagram 32). The green in-focus symbol lights to tell you if you have focused correctly.

You can use the manual setting after autofocusing to lock the focus – useful if you are firing the camera with a remote control, or taking a self-portrait.

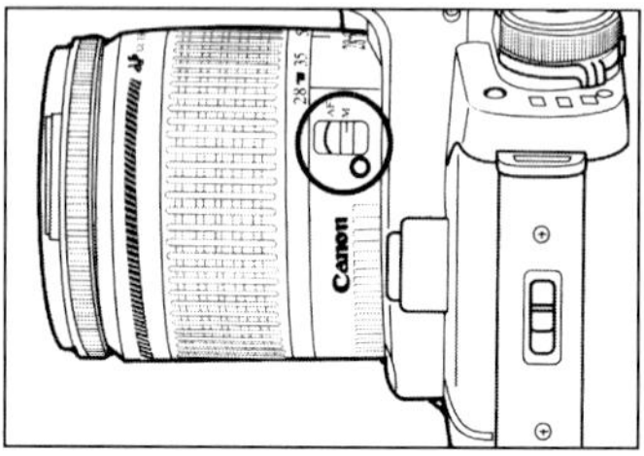

Diagram 31: *Slide the switch on the side of the lens to set Manual focus.*

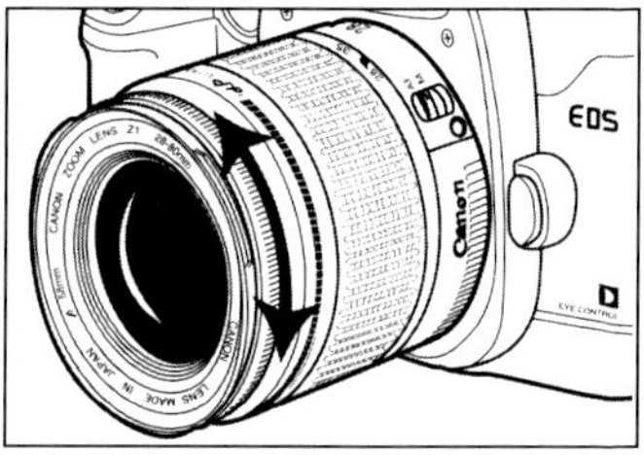

Diagram 32: *Turn the end of the lens to focus manually.*

Limits to autofocus

The EOS autofocus system is excellent. In most situations it focuses faster and more accurately than you could do manually. However, it does have limitations.

Rather like your eyes, the camera has to be able to 'see' what it is focusing on. In other words, the subject needs to have some contrast to it. The camera will struggle to focus on a plain white wall, sky or flat water. If your EOS 50/E – Elan II/E is unable to focus, try pointing it at a part of the subject that is the same distance away, but has more contrast, and then use Focus Lock while recomposing the picture. If this fails, switch to manual focus.

If you are photographing something through wire mesh or bars – such as a caged animal – the camera may focus on this rather than the subject. Switching to manual focus point selection may solve the problem, but if not, use manual focusing.

Whatever focus mode you are using, keep an eye on the viewfinder image to ensure that the camera is focusing where you want it to. If it is not, use Focus Lock, manual Focus Point selection, or manual focusing to override the camera.

Chapter Ten

Multipoint focusing

Your EOS 50/E – Elan II/E features a three-point focusing system. Most cameras simply focus on the centre of the viewfinder image, but this is no good if the subject is to one side of the frame; which is where you will often want to put it for a balanced composition.

The three-point system allows you to focus on a subject in the centre of the frame, or to one side or the other of the centre. The focus point can either be chosen automatically by the camera, manually by you, or in the case of the EOS 50E – Elan IIE, by Eye-control.

Automatic point selection

Automatic point selection is always used in Full Auto mode, it can also be selected in other shooting modes. Automatic point selection assumes that the area closest to the camera is the part of the scene that you wish to be in focus. If you think about it, most of your photographs have the main subject in the foreground.

Although this system is ideal for most photographs, it may not always give the result that you desire. For instance, you may be photographing a landscape framed by trees. In this situation the camera would focus on the trees rather than the main part of the scene. So it is important to always keep an eye on the area that the camera is focusing on. The selected focus point flashes red when the camera focuses. If the camera is not doing what you want, switch to Manual or Eye-control, or use Focus Lock.

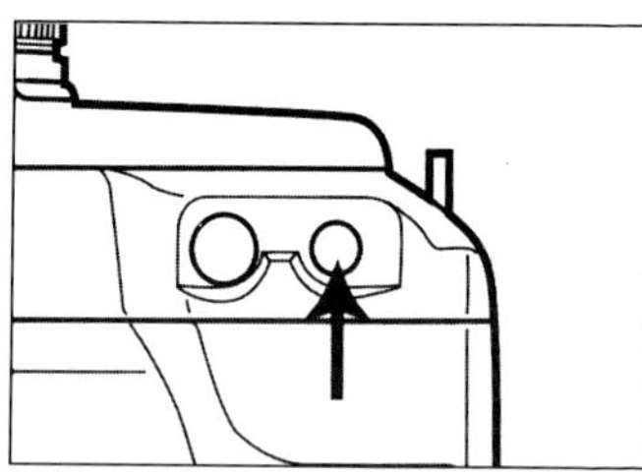

Diagram 33: *Press the Focus Point Select button to change focus points.*

To set Automatic point selection, make sure the camera is in a Creative Zone setting. Press and release the Focus Point Select button (Diagram 33) and, within six seconds, turn the Electronic Input Dial until all three focus points appear in the viewfinder and LCD panel.

Manual point selection

Manual point selection allows you to choose a focus point yourself. The selected point remains active until you change it, or switch to another selection method.

This can be useful in some situations. For instance, in sports photography the main subject is likely to be always in the centre of the frame, so you can select the centre focus point and switch off the outer two. Alternatively, with practice you can quickly switch from one point to another as you are composing a shot.

To manually select a focus point, press the Focus Point Select button and turn the Electronic Input Dial until the desired point flashes in the viewfinder and LCD panel. Remember to return the camera to your normal selection method after you have finished.

Eye-control selection : EOS 50E – Elan IIE only

The 'E' in EOS 50E – Elan IIE stands for Eye-control. The camera features an exciting Eye-control Focus system that was first seen on the EOS 5 (EOS A2E).

Eye-control Focus lets you use your eye to select the focus point. Simply glance at the focus point you wish to use and the camera focuses on the area covered by that point. This is faster than selecting the focus point manually, and gives you more control than automatic point selection.

The EOS 5 (EOS A2E) Eye-control system is very good, but only works when the camera is held horizontally. Canon refined the system for the EOS 50E – Elan IIE and it now works when the camera is held horizontally, vertically, or even upside down!

Calibrating Eye-control

Because there is no such thing as a standard eye, the EOS 50E – Elan IIE must be calibrated to recognise the unique characteristics of your eye. Once the initial calibration is completed, the camera has a self-learning system that continues to analyse your eye to fine-tune the setting.

So that you can let friends and family use your camera, the EOS 50E – Elan IIE has three calibration settings that allow up to three people to store their eye characteristics in the camera.

Calibration is straightforward and should be carried on in normal shooting conditions. If you use spectacles, make sure that you are wearing them during calibration. Likewise, if you use a dioptre correction lens, this should be attached to the camera. Although Eye-control works with either spectacles or dioptre correction lenses, do not attempt to use both – the camera will be unable to cope with it.

Turn the main Command Dial to 'CAL' (Diagram 34). 'CAL' and a number will appear in the LCD panel. This is the calibration setting, turn the Electronic Input Dial to set '1', '2' or '3' (Diagram 35). If no calibration settings have been previously stored, the numbers flash.

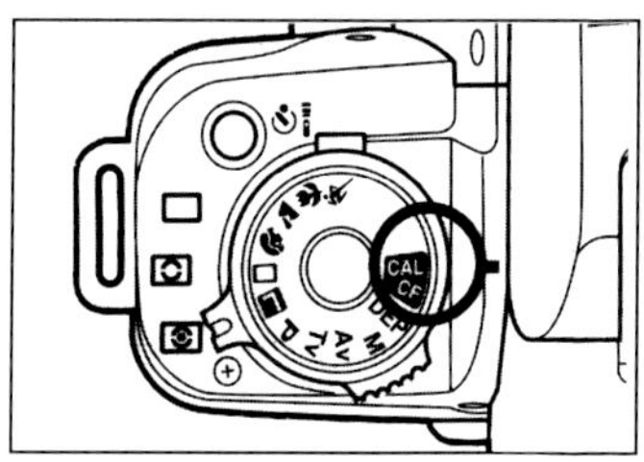

Diagram 34: *Turn the main Command Dial to 'CAL' to calibrate the Eye-control system.*

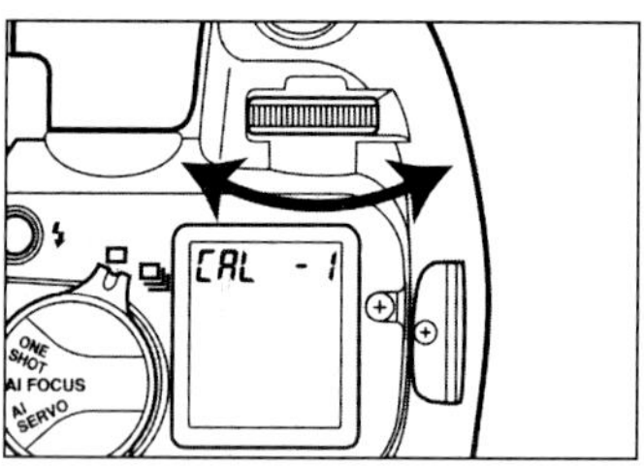

Diagram 35: *Turn the Electronic Input Dial to choose a calibration number – 1, 2 or 3.*

Look through the viewfinder. The right-hand focus mark will be flashing red. Look directly at this mark and fully press the shutter button. If the sound function is turned on, the camera will beep.

The left-hand focus mark will now flash. Look at this and press the shutter button, a beep will sound. The camera is calibrated for horizontal use.

Press the shutter button halfway and turn the camera to a vertical format. Look through the viewfinder and look at the top focus mark, which will be flashing red. Press the shutter button and a beep will sound (whichever way you hold the camera, the top focus mark flashes).

The bottom focus mark will now flash red. Look at this and press the shutter button again. A beep will be heard and 'End' will appear in the LCD panel. Your EOS 50E – Elan IIE is fully calibrated.

If you do not look directly at the flashing focus mark during calibration, the camera will beep continuously and the LCD panel will flash. Press the shutter button and start the process again.

Now that you have calibrated the camera to your eyesight, do not let other people use it with your setting. The self-learning feature is confused by different eyes and the accuracy of Eye-control will be affected. If you find that the system is not working as well as you expect, delete the setting and start again. To do this, turn the main Command Dial to 'CAL' and rotate the Electronic Input Dial until your number appears in the LCD panel. Now press simultaneously the AE Lock and Focus Point Select buttons. The calibration number will blink.

Using Eye-control

Eye-control Focus is possible in all shooting modes except Full Auto and Depth. To set Eye-control, press the Focus Point Select button and turn the Electronic Input Dial until the eye symbol appears in the LCD panel and viewfinder.

When you look through the viewfinder, simply glance at the focus point that you wish to use and half-press the shutter button to focus. The selected point flashes red and the lens focuses on the area covered by the point.

Occasionally, the camera is unable to recognise where your eye is looking. If this happens, it switches to automatic point selection and focuses on the area closest to the camera. The viewfinder Eye-control symbol flashes to warn you that this has occurred.

Chapter Eleven
Film winding and rewinding

In the old days, photographers had to wind on the film manually between frames, either by turning a knob, or cocking a lever. Although hardly strenuous, this did slow down the picture-taking process and meant that there was a risk that the camera was not always ready for action.

The EOS 50/E – Elan II/E uses a motor to automatically wind on the film after each exposure. After all the frames have been exposed, another motor rewinds the film into its cassette ready for removal.

Depending on the type of pictures you are taking, you can choose from two different winding modes. These are set by the peripheral control of the second Command Dial (Diagram 36).

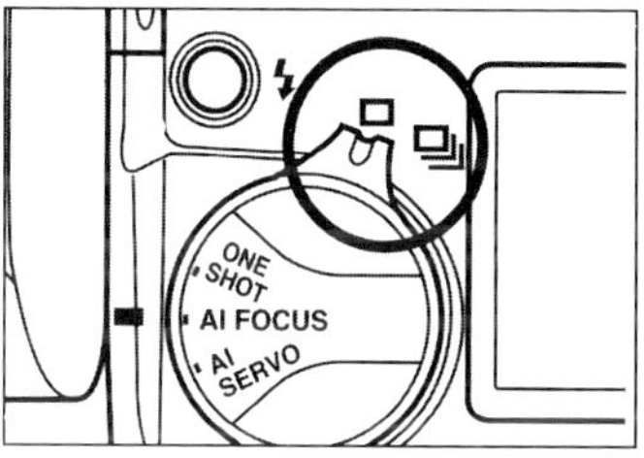

Diagram 36: *Turn the peripheral control of the second Command Dial to set the film winding mode.*

Single exposure □

Single exposure is the mode to use for most of your pictures. When you fully press the shutter button, the camera takes a picture and winds on the film to the next frame ready for your next shot. But you then have to either take your finger off the shutter button or release the button to its halfway position before you can take another photograph. This is a safety device to stop you from accidentally shooting a number of frames by not releasing the button quick enough.

Single exposure mode is ideal when you just want to take one picture at a time. Use it for static subjects such as buildings and landscapes. It is also a good idea to set this mode to avoid wasting film when a novice is using the camera.

Continuous exposure

In Continuous exposure mode, the camera winds on the film and fires the shutter for as long as the shutter button is depressed. With a fresh battery in the camera, this means that you can take a photograph about every 2.5 seconds, and use a 24-exposure film in one minute.

Continuous exposure mode is used for action photography when you want to ensure that you capture the definitive moment. For instance, if you were photographing a racing car flying around a corner, you would press the shutter button just as the car reached the bend and hold it down as the vehicle negotiated the corner. The resulting sequence of pictures would show the car at various points on the curve, allowing you to choose the most suitable after the film is processed.

Many people like to use Continuous mode for portrait and fashion photography because it allows them to take a series of pictures as the model moves around.

Use Continuous exposure mode with care – it can prove costly in terms of film!

Film rewind

The EOS 50/E – Elan II/E automatically rewinds the film at the end of a roll. Normally, rewind is almost silent. However, setting Custom Function 1 to ‘1’ increases the rewind speed, but the motor is slightly noisier. Choose the setting that suits the situation you are in.

Mid-roll rewind

Sometimes, you may wish to remove a film before it is finished. For instance, if you have been using a colour slide film, but wish to shoot some black-and-white shots. You could just waste the remaining frames in the slide film, but it is more frugal to wind the film back into its cassette to be used at a later date.

To do this, press the mid-roll rewind button on the back of the camera – it is recessed so that it cannot be pressed accidentally (Diagram 37). The film will then rewind into its cassette; the film counter in the LCD panel counts down as this happens.

The problem with doing this is that the film leader is also wound into the cassette, making it impossible to reload. You can buy a little film retriever that hooks the end of the film from the cassette, but there is a risk that doing this will scratch the delicate emulsion. It is far better to set Custom Function 2 to '1'. This tells the camera to leave the film leader exposed.

After taking a part-used film out of the camera, it is important to mark it clearly so that you don't mistake it for an unexposed film – note the number of frames that have been shot.

When you come to reuse a part-used film, you must wind it on to the first unexposed frame. To do this, set the camera and lens to Manual and choose a shutter speed of 1/4000 second and the smallest possible aperture. Put a lens cap over the lens and keep away from bright light. Now fire the shutter until the film counter in the LCD panel reaches the point that you took the film out at. Fire an extra frame just to make sure. The reason for doing it this way is to minimise the risk of light entering the camera when you fire the shutter. If you tried to fire the shutter with a lens cap on in an automatic shooting mode, the camera would try to give a correct exposure and make the shutter stay open for 30 seconds. The lens must be set to Manual otherwise the camera will try, and fail, to autofocus and the shutter will lock.

Diagram 37: *Press the Mid-roll rewind button on the back of the camera to rewind a part-used film.*

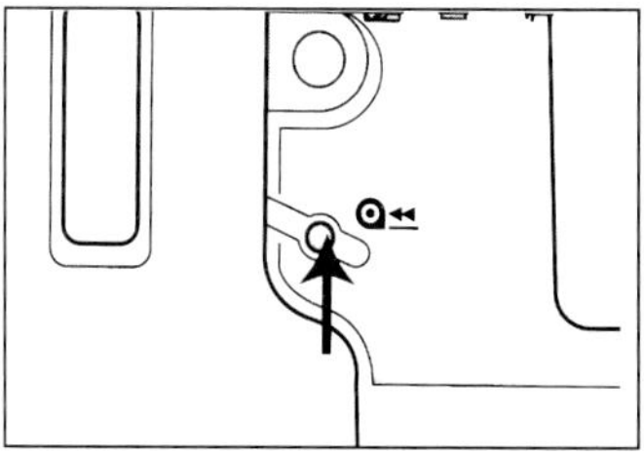

Chapter Twelve
Multiple exposures

An interesting feature of the EOS 50/E – Elan II/E is the Multiple Exposure facility. Normally, your camera only allows you to expose each frame once – as soon as you have taken a photograph, the film winds on to the next frame ready for the next shot. However, in Multiple Exposure mode, the film wind is cancelled, allowing you to make a number of exposures on a single frame. This gives you the ability to take a range of special effect photographs.

Setting Multiple Exposure

It is not possible to shoot multiple exposures when the camera is set to Full Auto or a PIC mode, so choose a Creative Zone setting.

Press the Function button on the back of the camera until the Multiple Exposure symbol appears in the LCD panel. A number '1' will also appear (Diagram 38). Turn the Electronic Input Dial to change this to the number of exposures you wish to make on a single frame – up to nine can be set.

When you now press the shutter button fully to take a photograph, the shutter will open but the film will not wind on until you have made the preset number of exposures. During the sequence, the Multiple Exposure symbol will flash in the LCD panel and the number of remaining exposures is displayed. After all the exposures have been made, the camera reverts to normal operation; if you wish to take another multiple exposure photograph, you will have to make the setting again.

To cancel Multiple Exposures, press the Function button until the symbol appears in the LCD panel, and turn the Electronic Input Dial to return the number of exposures to one.

Although it is very unlikely that you will want to, it is possible to make more than nine exposures on a single frame. When the set number of exposures reaches one, press the Function button and turn the Electronic Input Dial to increase the number of exposures and then start shooting again. You can do this as many times as you like to give an unlimited number of exposures!

There is no limit to how long you can wait between exposures during a sequence – you can leave the camera for hours, minutes, weeks or even months between making one exposure and the next. Just remember that Multiple Exposure mode is set and don't try to use the camera for anything else. You can also change lenses and add a Speedlite or a filter between exposures. It is possible to change shooting modes, but do not try and set Full Auto or a PIC mode – this will cancel Multiple Exposure mode.

__Diagram 38:__ Press the Function button until the Multiple Exposure symbol appears in the LCD panel, together with a number '1'.

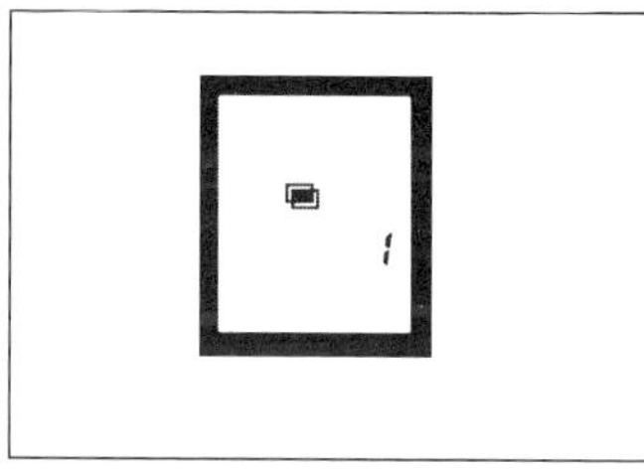

Using Multiple Exposure mode

Before using Multiple Exposure mode you need to decide what film winding mode to use. Single frame is best if you want to wait some time between exposures, whereas Continuous mode allows you to make all the exposures in quick succession.

If you are exposing the same scene more than once on the same frame, the film will receive too much light. To avoid this happening, decrease each exposure using Exposure Compensation (see Chapter 8). The amount of compensation required increases with the number of exposures and depends on the type of subject you are photographing. However, as a guide, set Exposure Compensation to -1 stop for two exposures, -1.5 stops for three exposures and -2 stops for four exposures.

What is Multiple Exposure mode for?

Multiple Exposure mode allows you to create all sorts of interesting and unusual effects. Here are just some ideas, you should be able to think of many more.

Make a ghost image

If you want to make your friends believe that you have seen a ghost, try this simple technique.

Mount your camera on a tripod or other firm surface and set Multiple Exposure mode to two and Exposure Compensation to -1. Press the shutter button once and then get someone to step into the scene before making the second exposure.

When the film is processed you will see that the person appears transparent. This is because the first background was exposed to the film for the first exposure and then the person was exposed over the top.

If your friends aren't convinced by this, try putting a white sheet over your subject!

Add the moon to a scene

You have probably seen landscape photographs featuring a huge moon. It looks impressive, but never happens in reality – if you tried to shoot such a scene, the moon would appear far too small.

The answer is to photograph the landscape and the moon separately, using a telephoto lens for the moon shot. To be successful, the landscape must be photographed in low light so that the sky appears dark, otherwise you will get a see-through moon!

Create twins

It is possible to include the same person twice on one frame. However, if you just make two exposures with the subject in a different place, you will end up with the ghost effect described earlier. The answer is to mask half of the lens so that only half of the frame is exposed at a time. Special masks are available to fit square filter systems – your local photo dealer will be able to get you a set.

To use the mask, mount your camera on a tripod and put the mask over one side of the lens. Look through the viewfinder; you will see that half of the frame is blacked out. Ask your subject to stand on the other side so that you can see them in the viewfinder. Set Multiple Exposure mode to two and make the first exposure (you do not need to set Exposure Compensation because each half of the film is only being exposed once). Taking care not to move the camera, move the mask to the other side of the lens and ask your subject to move across so that they appear on the other side of the viewfinder, then make the second exposure.

Chapter Thirteen
Custom Functions

Your EOS 50/E – Elan II/E is designed to be easy for any photographer to use, from beginners to professionals. But everyone is different and we all want different things from a camera. Which is why the EOS 50/E – Elan II/E has Custom Functions. These allow you to customise the camera to suit your specific needs. A number of aspects of camera operation can be altered using Custom Functions, including film rewind, exposure metering and flash characteristics. You can choose to ignore Custom Functions, and use the camera as it left the factory, or set one or more as you please. You can also set different Custom Functions for different types of photography.

Warning

Custom Functions offer a powerful way of altering the operation of your EOS 50/E – Elan II/E. But use them with care. It is easy to forget that you have set a Custom Function and then wonder why your camera is not operating as you expect.

If you think that your EOS 50/E – Elan II/E is faulty, run through the Custom Functions to see which ones have been set. Also, if you lend the camera to anyone, check the Custom Functions when you get it back to make sure that they are set as you like them.

Setting Custom Functions

To set a Custom Function, turn the Main Command Dial to 'CF' (Diagram 39). The symbol 'CF' will appear in the LCD panel. Turn the Electronic Input Dial until the desired Custom Function number appears after the letter 'C' in the LCD panel. Now press the Custom Function setting button (inner one on the back of the camera behind the LCD panel) until the required setting number for that Custom Function appears in the LCD panel. Set it to '0' to return the camera to the default setting.

When you have finished setting Custom Functions, turn the main Command Dial to another position to store the settings.

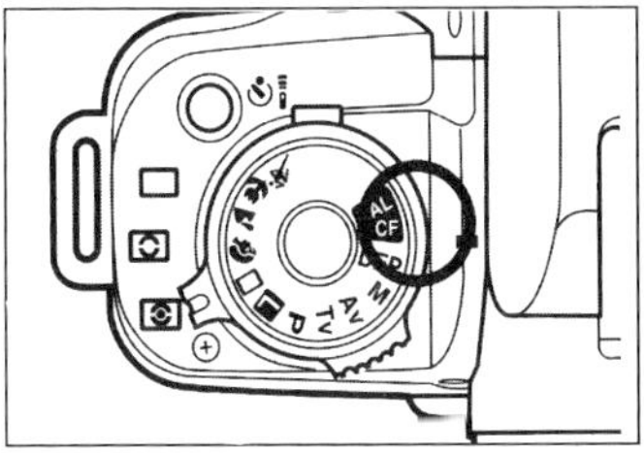

Diagram 39: *Turn the Command Dial to 'CF' to set Custom Functions.*

Custom Function 1 - film rewind

This controls film rewind at the end of a film, and allows you to make the most of the camera's quiet mechanism. Silent rewind is slower but quieter than highspeed.

0 – Silent rewind
1 – Highspeed rewind

Custom Function 2 – film leader

This lets you choose to leave the film leader outside the cassette after rewind – a useful feature for photographers who process their own films, or for rewinding a part-used film that you wish to finish at a later date. If you set this Custom Function, make sure that you have a system of identifying exposed films so that you do not accidentally reload them.

0 – Rewinds the film leader into cassette
1 – Leaves the film leader exposed

Custom Function 3 – film speed setting

Normally, the EOS 50/E – Elan II/E reads the DX Code on a film cassette and automatically sets the film speed. If you always rate your films at a different speed to that recommended by the manufacturer, or use non-DX Coded films, this Custom Function cancels automatic film speed setting. Use it with care and remember to reset it to 0 if you wish to take advantage of DX Coded film. Turn to Chapter 3 to find out how to manually set the film speed.

0 – Automatic DX film speed setting
1 – Manual film speed setting

Custom Function 4 – AE Lock, autofocus activation, depth-of-field preview

Some people have difficulty pressing the shutter button halfway to activate autofocus. This Custom Function lets you use the AE Lock button on the back of the camera to activate autofocus. It also lets you use the AE Lock button as a depth-of-field preview button (see Chapter 6). Note that, unlike other Custom Functions, this one has three options. Also, setting 1 or 2 disables FE Lock when using the Speedlite 380EX.

0 – Autofocus activated by shutter button. AE Lock activated by the AE Lock button
1 – Autofocus activated by the AE Lock button. AE Lock activated by the shutter button
2 – Autofocus activated by shutter button. Pressing AE Lock button activates depth-of-field preview

Custom Function 5 – mirror lock

If you undertake high magnification macro work at long shutter speeds, the movement of the mirror rising just before the exposure may cause camera shake to spoil the photograph. When the self-timer is set, this Custom Function gives a two second delay between the mirror rising and the shutter firing – enough for any movement to subside. Can be used with Remote Control RC-1.

0 – Normal self-timer operation
1 – Mirror rises two seconds before the shutter fires in self-timer mode.

Custom Function 6 – flash synchronisation

This allows you to change the synchronisation of either the built-in flash or a Speedlite 380EX. In first curtain sync, the flash fires at the beginning of an exposure – as soon as the shutter is fully open. However, there are times when you will get a better result if the flash fires at the end of the ambient exposure – just before the shutter closes. This is second curtain sync.

At fast shutter speeds you will not notice any difference between first and second curtain sync. However, during long shutter speeds a moving subject can travel some distance in the time that the shutter is open. During first curtain synchronisation, the flash captures the subject as a sharp image at the start of its travel across the film. When second curtain sync is set, the sharp image is made after the movement has been captured on film, this is a more natural effect because it gives a suggestion of movement.

0 – First curtain synchronisation
1 – Second curtain synchronisation

Custom Function 7 – auxiliary focusing light

In low light, the camera emits a beam of light to illuminate the subject and aid focusing. This Custom Function allows you to disable the auxiliary focusing light, which can be useful in situations where other people are taking photographs and the light may spoil their pictures.

0 – Auxiliary focusing light enabled
1 – Auxiliary focusing light disabled

Custom Function 8 – Partial metering and FE Lock

Normally, Partial and FE Lock readings are taken from just the centre focus point. However, this Custom Function allows you to link the reading to any focus point during manual point selection (when automatic focus point selection is set, this Custom Function does not operate).

0 – Partial and FE Lock meter reading taken from the centre focus point
1 – Partial and FE Lock meter reading taken from the active focus point

Custom Function 9 – shutter speed setting in Aperture Priority flash photography

When taking flash photographs in Aperture Priority mode, the camera sets a shutter speed that will ensure a correct ambient exposure. At small apertures in dim conditions, this can result in a long shutter speed being set. If this happens, you need to set the camera on a tripod to avoid camera shake spoiling the picture. However, setting this Custom Function locks the shutter speed at 1/125 second (the maximum sync speed), which may underexpose the background but will leave the flash exposure unaltered.

0 – Shutter speed set according to ambient light
1 – Shutter speed locked at 1/125 second

Custom Function 10 – focus points

You may find the flashing focus points irritating, especially when you are focusing manually. This Custom Function allows you to turn them off.

0 – Focus points flash on completion of focusing
1 – Focus points do not flash on completion of focusing.

Custom Function 11 – Eye-control depth-of-field preview

Only on the EOS 50E – Elan IIE, this Custom Function allows you to turn off the Eye-control depth-of-field preview facility.

0 – Eye-control depth-of-field preview enabled
1 – Eye-control depth-of-field preview disabled

Chapter Fourteen

Basic flash photography

An essential ingredient for a successful photograph is light. The film in your camera reacts to light and forms a latent image. This image then becomes visible when the film is processed.

The EOS 50/E – Elan II/E can still be used when the light drops. It has a small built-in flashgun that pops up from the top of the camera when it is needed. When you need more power, you can attach a dedicated Canon Speedlite to the camera. But don't think that flash can only be used in low light; later in this chapter we'll explain how flash can be used to improve your outdoor photographs.

If you have ever used flash with less sophisticated cameras you have probably been disappointed and frustrated by the results. Flash photography used to be a complex and often unreliable exercise. But the EOS 50/E – Elan II/E with either its built-in flash or a Speedlite makes flash photography straightforward and accurate.

This chapter explains briefly how to take flash photographs with your EOS 50/E – Elan II/E. If you have a Speedlite flashgun, you should also read the Hove Foto Books User's Guide to Canon Speedlites 420EZ, 430EZ and 540EZ.

What is TTL flash metering?

TTL stands for Through-The-Lens. A sensor inside the camera reads the amount of flash light that enters the camera lens and quenches the flash when enough light has been received for a correct exposure.

Simpler flash systems use a sensor on the front of the flashgun. The advantage of a TTL system is that it automatically compensates for filters, flash diffusers and bounced flash.

The Speedlite 540EZ features A-TTL flash metering in some modes; the A stands for Advanced. This system relies on a small preflash to determine the flash-to-subject-distance. Once the camera knows this, it sets an aperture that ensures a correct flash exposure and a correct ambient exposure, at all shooting distances within the range of the flash. The actual power of the flash is determined at the moment of exposure by a flash meter that measures the amount of light reflecting off the film surface.

The Speedlite 380EX, when attached to the EOS 50/E – Elan II/E, boasts E-TTL flash metering. This is an improvement of A-TTL metering that uses the camera's 6-zone Evaluative metering for the flash reading – E stands for Evaluative.

This system determines the flash exposure by giving a preflash a split-second before the exposure. At the same time, the camera measures the ambient light to ensure that both the ambient and flash exposures are correct and balanced. It also takes into account the active focus point and ensures that the part of the picture you are focusing on is correctly exposed.

The power of the flash is controlled not by its brightness, but by its duration – the longer the flash, the more powerful it is. The duration varies between 1/750 and 1/20,000 second, so all you will notice is that a long flash appears brighter than a short one.

At the end of the day, you do not need to know how TTL flash metering works, just that it creates great pictures!

Using the built-in flash

When your EOS 50/E – Elan II/E is set to Full Auto, Portrait or Close-up mode, the built-in flash pops up when the camera senses that it is needed. This may be when it is dark, or if the camera senses strong backlighting. Either way, the camera uses TTL flash metering to ensure a correct exposure. This is the easiest way to take snapshots and other snatch photographs. The flash never fires in Landscape or Sport modes.

In Creative Zone modes, the built-in flash only fires when you want it to. To activate the unit, press the flash button to the right of the pentaprism (Diagram 40).

Diagram 40: *Press the flash button to the right of the pentaprism to pop-up the built-in flash.*

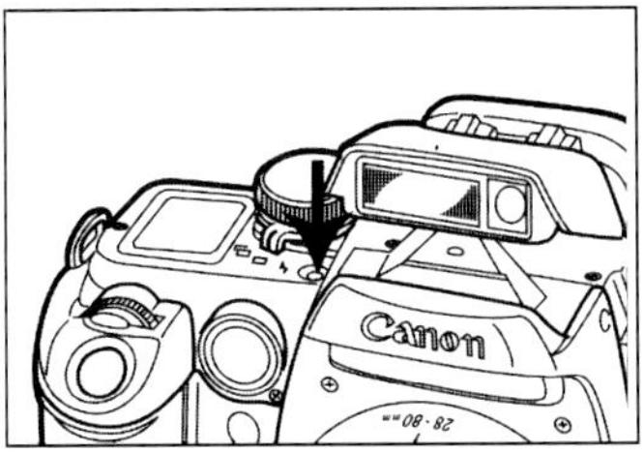

The built-in flash has a coverage equivalent to the angle-of-view of a 28mm lens. If you use it with wider focal lengths, the edges of the image will not be illuminated. There is not a problem using the flash with focal lengths greater than 28mm.

Do not attach a lens hood when using the built-in flash – the hood may obstruct the light from the flash and cause part of the subject to be in shadow. For the same reason, Canon EF lenses with an extremely wide front element cannot be used with the built-in flash. These lenses include the EF 20-35mm f2.8L and most super-telephoto white lenses.

The built-in flash cannot be activated when an external flashgun is attached to the camera. Some people put a plastic cover over the camera hotshoe; don't do this, it is not necessary and will stop the flash from popping-up.

Light from a flashgun falls away with distance. Imagine driving on a dark night. Objects close to you are brightly lit by your car's headlamps, while those farther away remain in darkness until you get closer to them. The light from the built-in flash behaves in the same way. The range of the flash depends partly on film speed, but generally speaking, for successful built-in flash photographs, you should ensure that the subject is no farther than four metres from you.

Remember that using the built-in flash increases drain on the camera battery, so don't use the flash if the subject is a long way from you. You have probably seen flashguns firing at concerts, many metres from the performers. That is a waste of time; you either need to use a very fast film, or set a long shutter speed to ensure a good result in such situations.

The built-in flash can cause harsh shadows if the subject is in front of a wall. To avoid this happening, try to ensure your subject is some way in front of walls and other surfaces. Also, the direct flash can reflect off spectacles and windows. Ask your subject to take off their spectacles or look downwards. The easiest way to avoid reflections off windows is to close the curtains!

Don't be tempted to use flash for all your indoor photographs. If the room is attractively lit, the flash can destroy the ambience. If in doubt, take two photographs – one with flash and a second without.

Red-eye and the built-in flash

You have probably seen snapshots of people with glaring red eyes – a common problem with flash photographs. It is caused when bright light enters the eye – such as that from a direct flashgun – and is reflected off the blood vessels of the retina and coloured red by them. This leads to the distinctive red-glow in the subject's eyes.

Red-eye is most likely to occur in dark conditions when the subject's pupils expand to let more light in. Children's pupils take longer to contract than adults and therefore are more susceptible to the problem.

Alcohol affects the reaction time of a person's pupils, which is one reason why red-eye often occurs on pictures taken at parties or down the pub!

Red-eye may also occur when you are photographing animals – especially nocturnal ones such as cats and foxes. These creatures have large pupils to enable them to see in dark conditions, which means that more light can enter and bounce off the retina. What's more, an animal's eyes may end up appearing green or yellow instead of red! This is because they have a less developed retina that reflects light in a different way. You may have experienced this effect when driving along a dark road – animal eyes caught in the beam from your car's headlights develop a sinister glow.

The problem of red-eye occurs when the flashgun is close to the camera's lens axis. Therefore, the built-in flash is more likely to cause red-eye than a Speedlite, which is mounted farther from the lens.

You may think that red-eye only occurs with colour film. You'd be right, but don't think that you will automatically avoid the problem by shooting in black-and-white. Obviously the eyes won't appear red on a monochrome print, but they may reproduce pale and milky – which can look even more spooky than red-eye!

Red-eye reduction lamp

Your EOS 50/E – Elan II/E has a red-eye reduction facility. This is a bright light that shines at the subject prior to the flash firing. The light causes the subject's pupils to contract, limiting the amount of light that can enter the eyes and therefore reducing the risk of red-eye occurring.

Red-eye reduction works well so long as the subject is looking directly at the camera while the light is lit. And that can be a problem – people often look away when a bright light is shone in their eyes!

To set red-eye reduction, press the Function button on the back of the camera until the red-eye reduction symbol appears in the LCD panel. Then turn the electronic Input Dial until '1' appears in the LCD panel.

To use red-eye reduction, activate the built-in flash and half press the shutter button; the red-eye reduction lamp will light and warning symbols appear in the LCD panel and viewfinder. After two seconds, press the shutter button all the way to take the photograph. You can fire the shutter before two seconds is up, but the red-eye reduction lamp may not have had time to be effective.

Other ways of avoiding red-eye

Red-eye in photographs is caused by flash (although very occasionally it can occur with other bright lights, such as a car's headlamps). So turn off the built-in flash and the problem goes away.

Of course, there are times when you have to use flash – if there is no available light, you have no choice but to activate the built-in unit. But sometimes the ambient light can be very attractive and may give better results than a flashgun. Remember to keep an eye on the shutter speed and be ready to use a tripod or monopod if it drops below hand-holding levels.

Red-eye is most likely to occur when the subject is looking straight at the camera. So ask them to look away from you while you take a photograph.

Don't think that portraits need to have the person looking straight at the camera. Often, you can achieve a more attractive photograph if your subject is looking into the distance, reading a book, or perhaps engaged in a favourite hobby.

In dim conditions, your pupils expand to let more light enter the eye and enable you to see better. This also lets in more light from a flash, therefore increasing the risk of red-eye. So if you increase the room lighting, your subjects' pupils will contract very quickly, making red-eye less of a problem.

Load a fast film (such as ISO 400). This requires less exposure and therefore the flash output will be less.

Red-eye is particularly troublesome with the built-in flash because it is so close to the lens axis. Treat yourself to a Canon Speedlite and the problem will reduce considerably. Adding a Sto-Fen diffuser to the Speedlite will practically eliminate the risk of red-eye. It will also reduce harsh shadows and reflections during flash photography. Ask your local photo dealer for details.

These techniques will ensure that red-eye does not spoil your photographs. But what about pictures that you already have? Before you throw away all your red-eye shots, treat yourself to a red-eye retouching pen. You can buy one from a photo dealer. It is basically a fibre-tip pen containing a special green ink. By following carefully the instructions that come with the pen, you can retouch the eyes and restore your family and friends to normal human beings.

A red-eye retouching pen will save your existing prints, but in future, remember that prevention is better than cure!

Using a Speedlite

Any EZ, EX or EG Canon Speedlite can be used with your EOS 50/E – Elan II/E. These include:

Speedlite 160E,	Speedlite 200E,
Speedlite 300EZ,	Speedlite 420EZ,
Speedlite 430EZ,	Speedlite 540EZ,
Speedlite 300EX, and	Speedlite 480EG.

The Macro Ring Lite ML-3 can also be used for close-up photography.

Here is a brief specification and description of the currently available models:

Speedlite 200E

The Speedlite 200E is really designed for EOS cameras that do not have a built-in flash, so it is unlikely that you will want to buy one for your EOS 50/E – Elan II/E.

Like an EOS built-in flash, the low-power Speedlite 200E offers one mode – TTL, making it ideal for straightforward flash photography. Used with an Off Camera Cord, the Speedlite 200E is ideal for macro photography.

Specification

Type: Direct flash only
Modes: TTL (200M; external flash sensor only)
Focal length coverage: 35mm (28mm with clip-on adaptor)
Maximum Guide Number (ISO 100, m): 20
Power Source: 4x AA cells
Weight: 130g (excluding batteries)
Size: 64x104x41mm
Introduced: 1990

Speedlite 380EX

The Speedlite 380EX is designed especially for use with the EOS 50/E – Elan II/E, although it can also be used with other EOS models. When used with the EOS 50/E – Elan II/E, it offers E-TTL flash metering, flash synchronisation at all shutter speeds in FP mode and FE Lock. The head tilts upwards, but does not swivel from side to side.

Specification
Type: Bounce
Modes: E-TTL, A-TTL, TTL FE Lock
Focal length coverage: 24-105mm, auto-zoom
Maximum Guide Number (ISO 100, m): 38
Power Source: 4x AA cells
Weight: 270g (excluding batteries)
Size: 80x138x112mm
Introduced: 1995

Speedlite 540EZ

The Speedlite 540EZ is a top-of-the-range flashgun with a range of features, including fill-in ratio control; manual power settings from 1/1 to 1/128 power and strobe flash frequencies up to 100Hz.

To avoid the flash 'missing' the subject during close-up photography, the bounce head can be tilted down 7°.

Specification
Type: Bounce and Swivel
Modes: A-TTL, TTL, Variable power manual
Focal length coverage: 24-105mm, auto-zoom with manual override
Maximum Guide Number (ISO 100, m): 54
Power Source: 4x AA cells, or external pack
Weight: 415g (excluding batteries)
Size: 80x138x112mm
Introduced: 1994

Speedlite 480EG

The Speedlite 480EG is a hammerhead flashgun for the professional or keen amateur photographer who demands a high flash output.

The 480EG does not offer full A-TTL flash metering. However, it can be used in TTL mode with all EOS cameras, as well as the T90. In addition, the 480EG has an external flash sensor so that it can be used with SLR cameras that do not offer TTL metering – the Canon F-1 or A-1, for example.

Specification

Type: Bounce and swivel hammerhead
Modes: TTL, External sensor, Manual
Focal length coverage: 35mm (20mm with Wide Panel, 135mm with Tele Panel)
Maximum Guide Number (ISO 100, m): 48
Power Source: Transistor Pack E or NiCad Pack TP
Weight: 715g (excluding batteries)
Size: 98x256.5x114.3mm (excluding bracket)
Introduced: 1993

Attaching a Speedlite

The hotshoe (sometimes called an accessory shoe) on top of your EOS 50/E – Elan II/E is designed specifically to hold a Speedlite.

Not only does the hotshoe hold the Speedlite firmly in the optimum place for even flash coverage, it also has a number of electrical contacts. These link the camera and flash so that they work together as a single unit.

The Speedlite 380EX, Speedlite 430EZ and Speedlite 540EZ have a locking pin that engages with a hole in the camera hotshoe. This ensures that the flashgun is securely mounted and cannot slip off. Turn the locking ring on the base of the Speedlite clockwise to lock it onto the camera. Turn it anticlockwise to remove the Speedlite.

Once the Speedlite is attached and switched on it will fire for all your photographs.

See the next chapter for more information on using a Speedlite with your EOS 50/E – Elan II/E.

Macro Ring Lite ML-3

The Macro Ring Lite ML-3 is designed for close-up and macro photography. The flash unit mounts on the end of the lens and gives a ring of light to ensure even illumination of close subjects.

TTL metering takes the guesswork out of macro flash photography, which used to involve complex calculations to allow for the close focusing.

If you take macro photography seriously, the ML-3 is an essential addition to your EOS outfit.

Specification

Type: Macro ring flash
Modes: TTL
Focal length coverage: 50mm for macro, 28mm for normal
Maximum Guide Number (ISO 100, m): 11
Power Source: 4x AA cells
Weight: Control unit - 235g (excluding batteries)
Flash unit - 115g
Size: Control unit - 74x60.5x106.5mm
Flash unit - 101x120.5x20.6mm
Introduced: 1989

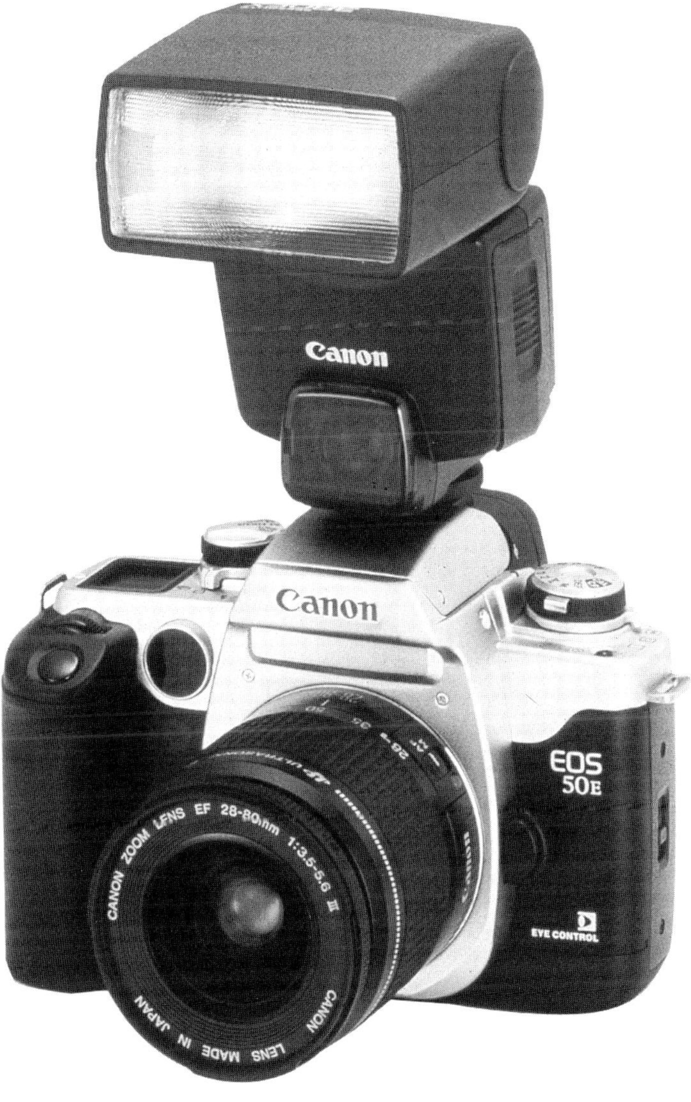

Canon EOS 50E - Elan IIE with Speedlite 380EX

Chapter Fifteen

Using flash

Flash in different shooting modes

Flash photography is possible in every shooting mode of your EOS 50/E – Elan II/E, but the results may be different in some modes to others. See Chapter 15 for information on flash in PIC modes.

Full Auto

In Full Auto mode, the built-in flash fires when the camera senses that it is needed. If a Speedlite is attached to your EOS 50/E – Elan II/E, it fires for every photograph, even if it's not strictly required. The shutter speed is set between 1/60 and 1/125 second to suit the ambient light.

Program Mode

In Program mode, the built-in flash must be activated manually by pressing the flash button, The camera sets a shutter speed between 1/60 and 1/125 second. The aperture is chosen according to subject distance – as calculated by the preflash – and ambient light level. This ensures a correct balance of ambient and flash exposures, down to a light level of EV10. At lower light levels, the ambient exposure is ignored to ensure that long shutter speeds are not set.

Shutter Priority mode

When using Shutter Priority, the built-in flash must be activated manually by pressing the flash button. With either the built-in flash or a Speedlite you are limited to a shutter speed of 1/125 second – the flash sync speed. If a shutter speed faster than the sync speed is set before the flash is turned on, the camera automatically overrides it and sets the sync speed.

The camera tries to set itself to give a correct exposure to the ambient light as well as the flash. If it is unable to do this, the viewfinder display will flash. You can ignore this and the flash exposure will be correct, but the background which is lit by daylight, might be underexposed.

The Speedlite 540EZ reverts to TTL mode when the camera is set to Shutter Priority mode.

Aperture Priority mode

You need to be careful using Aperture Priority mode with flash. The camera tries to ensure that the ambient exposure is correct, and as a result may end up setting a long shutter speed. You need to be aware of this and be ready to use a tripod if the shutter speed drops below hand-holding levels.

In bright light the camera may need to set a fast shutter speed to give a correct exposure, especially if you have chosen a wide aperture. However, when a Speedlite is attached, the camera is unable to set a speed faster than 1/125 second, in which case the picture may be overexposed. If this occurs, the shutter speed will flash in the viewfinder.

The Speedlite 540EZ reverts to TTL mode when the camera is set to Aperture Priority mode.

Manual mode

During flash photography, setting the camera to manual makes a difference to the flash metering system of Speedlites – A-TTL or E-TTL is replaced by TTL metering.

This can be very useful because the flashgun no long emits a preflash, which is a nuisance to wildlife photographers who do not want to scare their subjects, or to photojournalists taking candid shots.

Because there is no preflash, the camera cannot calculate the subject distance. Instead, the Speedlite displays the range that the flash will cover for the aperture, film speed and focal length you are using. So, as long as you know roughly how far you are from the subject, and you keep within the suggested range, you will get correctly exposed flash pictures. If your subject is beyond the indicated range, try setting a wider aperture, this will increase the flash range.

Note that the flash range is only displayed when the flash head is pointing forward, the values would not apply to bounce flash.

In Manual mode, you can set any shutter speed, including Bulb, up to 1/125 second – the flash sync speed. If a faster shutter speed is set, this will be overridden when the flash is activated.

When your EOS 50/E – Elan II/E is set to Manual it gives a guide to the ambient exposure in the viewfinder. You can use this to ensure that the background is correctly exposed, or ignore it and set a fast shutter speed and small aperture to give a dark background behind a subject correctly exposed by flash.

Depth mode

Flash should not be used in Depth mode. If you try to use either the built-in flash or a Speedlite, the camera will revert to Program mode.

Flash Exposure Compensation

During fill-in flash photography, your EOS 50/E – Elan II/E calculates what it thinks is a good balance between the flash and the ambient light. In most situations this is perfect, but there may be times when you want to alter this balance. Flash Exposure Compensation, also called Fill-in Ratio Control, is a feature of the EOS 50/E – Elan II/E that allows you to control the strength of either the built-in flash or certain dedicated Speedlites (only the Speedlite 380EX and models that offer fill-in ratio control on the flashgun).

Setting Flash Exposure Compensation

Make sure that the camera is set to a Creative Zone mode – compensation is not possible in Full Auto or PIC modes. Press the Function Button on the back of the camera until the Flash Exposure compensation symbol appears in the LCD panel (Diagram 41). Now turn the Electronic Input Dial or the Quick Control Dial (Diagram 42) until the desired amount of compensation appears on the scale in the LCD panel.

Flash Exposure Compensation remains set until you clear it, so make sure that you do not forget that you have used it. The symbol remains in the LCD panel to remind you.

If you are using a Speedlite 430EZ or Speedlite 540EZ, Flash Exposure Compensation can also be set on the Speedlite, this setting will override any made on the camera.

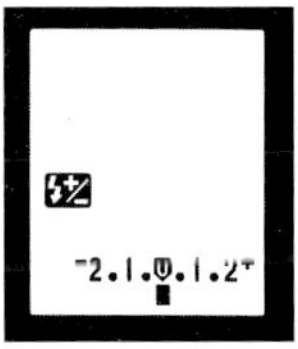

Diagram 41: *Press the Function button until the flash symbol appears in the LCD panel.*

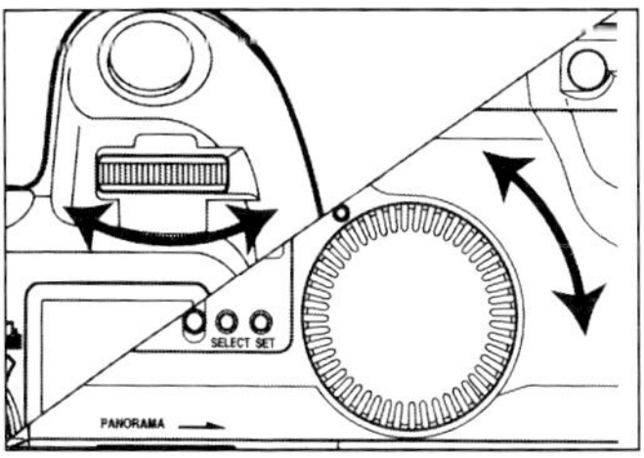

Diagram 42: *Set Flash Exposure Compensation by turning either the Electronic Input Dial or the Quick Control Dial.*

Combining flash and ambient Exposure Compensation

During fill-in flash photography, Flash Exposure Compensation affects only the flash exposure – the background, which is lit by ambient light, remains unaltered.

The EOS 50/E – Elan II/E Exposure Compensation control affects the total picture – that means that both the flash and the ambient exposures are increased or decreased by the amount you choose. However, if you use Exposure Compensation in conjunction with Flash Exposure Compensation, you can create some interesting effects and assume total control over your exposures.

Imagine that you are photographing a person outdoors in daylight, using flash to add light to their face. If you leave your camera to get on with it, you will get a quite natural looking photograph. However, say you want your subject to stand out against a dark background. In other words, you want the ambient light to be underexposed, while the flash exposure remains correct.

If you simply set the camera's exposure compensation to say, –3 stops, the whole photograph will be underexposed by that amount. This is where Flash Exposure Compensation comes in. Set it to +3 and the flash exposure will be increased by the same amount that the overall exposure has decreased. The result is a correct flash exposure in front of a dark background.

Because fill-in flash is abandoned when the light level drops below EV 10 in Program mode, it is best to use Aperture Priority mode for this technique – use a tripod or monopod if the shutter speed becomes too long for hand-held photography.

Chapter Sixteen
Using your EOS with studio flash

If you have a home studio, or are a professional photographer or member of a camera club, there is a good chance that you will want to connect your EOS 50/E – Elan II/E to studio flash units. These are large, powerful flash units mounted on stands. Unlike a Speedlite, studio flash units are manual only – they give out a fixed power flash and are not dedicated to the camera.

Although studio flash units do not have the sophistication of a Speedlite, they are more powerful. What's more, they feature modelling lamps. These are tungsten bulbs – rather like those in your home – that simulate the effect of the flash tube. In other words, the modelling lamps allow you to see what the lighting will look like so that you can make adjustments before firing the shutter – something that you cannot do with a Speedlite.

Studio flash units connect to the camera via a PC lead. No one is too sure what PC stands for. Some say it is short for Prontor Compur, the shutter manufacturers that designed the system. Others vote for Pin Cylinder, after the shape of the little plugs – the choice is yours. Either way, there is no denying that PC leads are a nuisance. The plugs are very small and not a positive fit. They date back to the days when flash leads plugged into a socket on the side of the lens where space was at a premium. The design became an almost universal standard, and today we are stuck with it.

Although the EOS 50/E – Elan II/E does not have a PC socket, you can still connect studio flash units, using an accessory called a hotshoe/PC adaptor – a little cube that fits onto the camera hotshoe and has a PC socket in the side. PC/Hotshoe adaptors are inexpensive, but also unreliable – they do not always form a good contact with the camera.

You can damage your camera by connecting an old-fashioned studio flash unit with a trigger voltage greater than 6v. However, modern equipment has a much lower trigger voltage and can be used quite safely.

Once you have done all this, there is a fair chance that the flash units will not fire when you press the shutter button! There are a number of reasons for this.

First, some types of studio flash, when used with Canon cameras, require a reverse polarity flash lead. This looks exactly the same as a normal flash lead, but the terminals on the plug are connected the other way around. Reverse polarity flash leads are available in the shops – Olympus OM cameras also use them. Or you can make your own – cut a normal PC lead, strip the wires and reconnect them the other way around.

Second, if the flash is not firing, try wiggling the adaptor around to see if you can make a contact.

Third, the flash lead may be too long. Leads longer than about 4 metres do not always work with EOS cameras. Also, multiple leads joined together can cause problems.

Last, the flash lead may be faulty! This is not uncommon. Most studios have a selection of leads, so try them one at a time.

If this all sounds like a lot of hassle – and it can be – there is an alternative. Most studio flash units have a slave cell. This is a light sensitive sensor that is triggered by the flash from another flashgun. All you have do is fit a Speedlite onto your camera, set it to low-power Manual, and bounce it off a wall or ceiling. The Speedlite will fire when you press the shutter, and activate the studio units. You may need to experiment with the angle of the Speedlite and the power setting. Remember that it is giving out a very low power flash compared to the studio units, and therefore will have little effect on the final photograph. And if you wonder if the studio flashes will fire quick enough to synchronise with the camera shutter, just think how fast light travels!

Setting the camera

Once you have connected your flash units, you must set your EOS 50/E – Elan II/E to Manual – you cannot use any other mode. In theory, you can use any shutter speed up to 1/125 second – the sync speed of the camera. However, in practice, some studio flash units do not fire as fast as a Speedlite and cannot synchronise with very short shutter speeds. Therefore, you should avoid setting shutter speeds faster than 1/90 second; remember that shutter speed has no effect on the flash exposure. Unlike using a Speedlite or built-in flash, when a non-dedicated flash unit is attached, the camera does not override shutter speeds faster than the sync speed – it is up to you to ensure that a suitable speed is set.

Aperture must be determined by a hand-held flash meter. Check that the meter is set to the correct film speed before taking a reading.

Chapter Seventeen
Self-timer operation

The self-timer feature of your EOS 50/E – Elan II/E puts a ten second delay between the shutter button being fully pressed and the shutter actually firing. The main use for this is for you to be able to include yourself in your photographs – handy for group shots that you want to be part of and times when you don't have anyone to take your photograph for you. However, the self-timer also has another use, as we shall find out.

Setting the self-timer

To set your EOS 50/E – Elan II/E to self-timer mode, all you have to do is press the self-timer button on the left-hand top plate (Diagram 43). The self-timer symbol will appear in the LCD panel. Now when the shutter button is depressed there will be a ten second delay before the shutter fires. You have four minutes after setting self-timer mode to press the shutter button; after this the camera reverts to normal operation.

To cancel self-timer mode, press the self-timer button again.

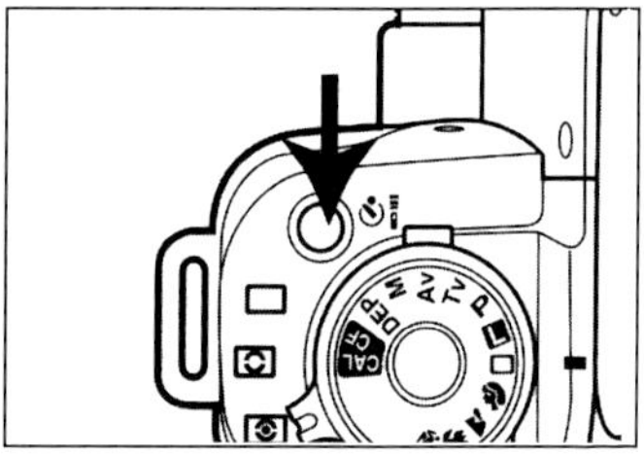

Diagram 43: *Press the self-timer button on the top of the camera to set it to self-timer mode.*

Using the self-timer

Any shooting mode can be used for self-timer photography. After setting self-timer mode, and within four minutes, press the shutter button halfway to focus and take an exposure reading. Now press the shutter button fully. The Auxiliary Focus light will flash and the camera will beep at 2Hz (twice a second) for eight seconds. During the last two seconds, the beeping and flashing increase to 8Hz (eight times a second) to warn you that shutter firing is imminent – time to smile! If the built-in flash is activated with red-eye reduction the red-eye reduction lamp will shine for the final two seconds.

Focusing

If you are using Eye-control focus, make sure that you are looking through the viewfinder when you half press the shutter button, to ensure that you select the desired focus point.

When taking a self-portrait, there is a risk that the camera will focus on the background and you will be out of focus. To avoid this happening, either get someone to stand in your place while you focus, or switch the lens to Manual focus and prefocus on the point where you will be standing. If there is enough light, set a small aperture so that there is plenty of depth-of-field to compensate for any slight focusing error.

Use a tripod

When using the self-timer, the camera must be firmly supported, ideally on a sturdy tripod; no you can't use a monopod! If you do not have a tripod handy, use a portable clamp, or place the camera on top of a wall, chair or table – look in the viewfinder to make sure that the surface does not appear in the picture. Make sure that the camera is safely supported – you don't want to see it toppling to the floor just before the shutter fires!

Eyepiece cover

Look at the strap that came with your EOS 50/E – Elan II/E. Where it changes from a thick to a thin section there is a piece of plastic (diagram 44). As well as being an integral part of the strap, this also acts as a viewfinder cover for self-timer operation.

This is necessary because, when your eye is not up to the camera, there is a slight risk that light will enter the viewfinder and affect the exposure reading. The eyepiece cover avoids this happening.

To use the eyepiece cover, first remove the rubber eyecup. You can then slide on the eyepiece cover – the cover remains on the strap.

For most of your self-timer photographs it is unlikely that stray light entering the viewfinder will adversely affect the exposure. However, if there is bright light shining directly into the viewfinder then it is a good idea to use the eyepiece cover.

Diagram 44: *Part of the strap doubles as an eyepiece cover.*

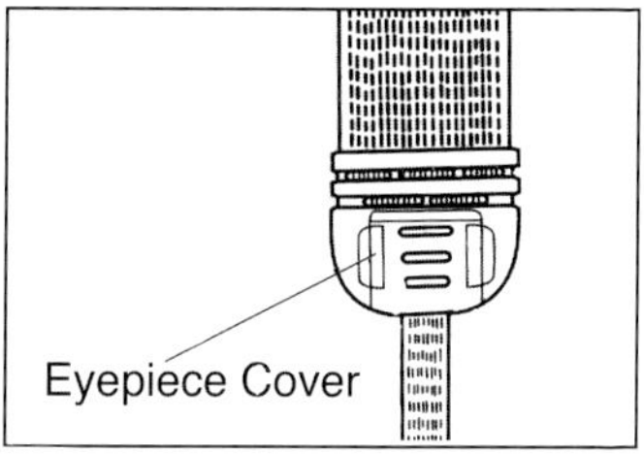

Use the self-timer to avoid camera shake

At the beginning of this chapter it was hinted that the self-timer was not just for taking self portraits. It can also help you avoid camera shake spoiling your photographs.

Even when the camera is mounted on a sturdy tripod, the act of pressing the shutter button can cause the camera to move slightly. At normal shutter speeds, this is not a problem, but during long exposures it can cause the image to be blurred.

One solution is to use a remote control (see Chapter 20), but if you do not have one handy, set the self-timer. The ten second delay is long enough for any movement caused by pressing the shutter button to subside.

This technique works well for inanimate objects, but is not suitable for moving subjects or situations when you need to fire the shutter at a precise moment.

Chapter Eighteen
Quartz Date models

The EOS 50/E – Elan II/E is available with a Quartz Date back that prints the date or time onto the film as you take a photograph. These models are designated 'QD'.

Unlike some EOS models, you cannot add the Quartz Date back to a normal EOS 50/E – Elan II/E, so when you buy your camera, think carefully whether or not you have a need for data imprinting; if you think you do, then go for the Quartz Date version.

How the Quartz Date back works

Inside the Quartz Date back is a tiny numerical Light Emitting Diode (LED) display behind the film pressure plate. This shines through the film onto the light sensitive emulsion where it causes a latent image to form. The colour of the LED display is such that the image on the processed film is orange, to stand out against most subjects. The data appears in the bottom right-hand corner of horizontal format photographs.

The Quartz Date back includes an electronic clock and calendar that ensure that the information printed on the film is accurate and you can see exactly when you took each photograph.

Setting the Quartz Date back

Before using the Quartz Date back, you must set it to the correct time and date. The procedure for this will be familiar to anyone who has set a digital watch or clock.

First, press the Mode button to display either the time or the date, depending on which you wish to set. Then press the Select button, a section of the read-out will flash. Press the Select button until the part of the read-out that you wish to alter flashes. Now press the Set button continuously until the correct reading appears. Press the Select button to store that setting and move on to the next part of the read-out. When the read-out is correct, press the Select button until the flashing stops.

From time to time, check that the time and date are correct. If you travel to another time zone you need to decide whether to reset the clock, or leave it on your home time zone.

Using the Quartz Date Back

By pressing the Mode button you can select five data imprinting options:

- — — — Data imprinting off (nothing printed onto film)
- 5 29 96 Date as month, day, year (May 29 1996)
- 29 5 96 Date as day, month, year (29 May 1996)
- 96 5 29 Date as year, month, day (1996 May 29)
- 29 14 30 Day and date as day, hour, minute (29th 2.30pm)

If you wish to use date imprinting, choose a format that you understand and always use the same one.

Having the data printed on all your pictures can be annoying, so remember to turn off the feature when you do not require it – always check to see if data imprinting is on before you start shooting. Some people just imprint the date onto the first frame of each film, or at the start of the day, which is often enough to help you to keep a shooting record.

When you are using data imprinting, bear in mind that the information is going to be in the bottom right corner of each horizontal photograph, and in either the top right or bottom left of vertical pictures, depending on which way you hold the camera. A solution is to move back slightly to leave a border around your picture that can be cropped out afterwards. Alternatively, take two versions of the picture – one with data imprinting and a second without.

Replacing the Quartz Date back battery

The Quartz Date back has its own power supply that powers the clock and calendar. This lasts about three years, after which the LCD panel on the back will start to fade.

To replace the battery, first check that you do not have a film loaded. Open the camera back and look at the inside of it by the hinge. You will see an arrow pointing at a little silver screw. Use a tiny screwdriver to remove this screw and the battery compartment lid will come loose. Remove it and hook the battery out. Put in a fresh battery and replace the cover. Finally put back and tighten the little screw. If you are not confident about doing this, take the camera to your local Canon dealer for help.

The time and date must be reset after replacing the battery.

Chapter Nineteen
Canon EF lenses

Until recently, most SLR cameras were sold with what is called a standard 50mm lens. The idea was that the lens had a similar angle-of-view to the human eye. In fact, most of us have an angle-of-view which is closer to a 35mm lens, but a 50mm lens was useful for general photography.

In recent years, the quality of zoom lenses has improved to such an extent that the 50mm lens has been replaced by the standard zoom lens – one with a range that includes the 50mm setting. You probably bought your EOS 50/E – Elan II/E with an EF 28-80mm f3.5-5.6 III USM.

Although a standard zoom is an ideal first lens and copes with most picture-taking situations, there will come a time when you want to add to your lens armoury. Maybe you want to get closer to distant objects, or include more in the frame. Before looking at the options available, let's find out more about Canon EF lenses.

Why buy a Canon lens?

Lenses that will fit onto your EOS 50/E – Elan II/E are made not only by Canon, but also by independent lens manufacturers. Although some of these are very good, others are not. Canon has a reputation to maintain so all of its lenses offer excellent optical quality.

Most of today's Canon EF lenses boast Ultrasonic focus motors, although other manufacturers have tried to copy this system, there is no doubt that the original is fastest, quietest and best.

If you buy a Canon lens you can be sure that it will be fully compatible, not only with your EOS 50/E – Elan II/E, but also with future EOS models. There have been compatibility problems with some independent lenses.

Although an independent lens may be cheaper to buy, don't forget that its resale value is likely to be much less than a comparable Canon optic. Canon lenses always command good second-hand prices.

Lens motors

Your EOS 50/E – Elan II/E has a built-in autofocus system. This sends signals to a motor in the lens that drives the lens elements in and out until the image is in focus. When autofocus cameras were in their infancy, most manufacturers chose to put the focus motor in the camera body. This meant that you did not have to buy a lens with each motor, but there had to be a mechanical link between the camera and lens.

Canon's engineers were not happy with this concept, they wanted a totally electronic lens mount without any moving parts that could go wrong. What's more, a mechanical linkage absorbs energy and makes focusing slower and less accurate. Another reason that Canon rejected the camera body lens motor system is that different lenses require different power motors. A wide-angle lens is lighter and has less distance to travel than does a super-telephoto lens. Canon's system means that each lens can be fitted with the optimum motor.

Early Canon EF lenses use Arc Form Drive, or AFD, motors. This works in the same way as conventional electric motors but, as its name suggests, it is in the shape of an arc so that it follows the contours of the lens barrel. AFD motors make a slight noise as they focus the lens, but for most people this sound is not obtrusive.

Some Canon lenses still use AFD motors, but most now feature the almost silent Ultrasonic motor, or USM. These lenses are identified by the initials 'USM' after the lens description, and also by an 'Ultrasonic' logo on the side of the barrel. Unlike ordinary electric motors, USMs use ultrasonic vibrations from piezoelectric elements. These vibrations cause the motor to rotate.

Not only are USM lenses silent, they are also faster than AFD powered optics.

Some popular Canon lenses use a Micro USM drive, also called Micro Motor, or MM. These offer the same performance as conventional USMs, but are more compact.

One or two low-cost Canon EF lenses feature a simple DC motor that is slower and noisier than a USM, but quite adequate as an entry-level lens.

All Canon EF lenses contain a second motor, this drives the aperture diaphragm. It is a stepping motor, which means that each time it receives an electric pulse from the camera, it moves one step. So by sending a number of pulses, the camera can control exactly how far the motor travels, and therefore accurately set the aperture.

The diaphragm motor is activated as you press the shutter button to take a photograph, so that the aperture is stopped down to the predetermined amount. It is also used to stop down the aperture during depth-of-field preview.

Focal length

The focal length of a lens is an important part of its description. It is defined as the distance between the rear nodal point of the lens and the film plane, when the lens is set to infinity, and is expressed in millimetres. But don't worry, you don't have to get a tape measure out to find out focal length – just look at the words around the front element. A short focal length, such as 28mm has a wider angle-of-view than does a long focal length lens, such as 200mm. A long focal length lens makes distant objects appear closer, while a short focal length takes in more of a scene.

Maximum aperture

Also written on the front of every Canon EF lens is an aperture value. This is the maximum aperture of the lens. Choose a lens with a wide maximum aperture, for instance f1.8, for low light photography.

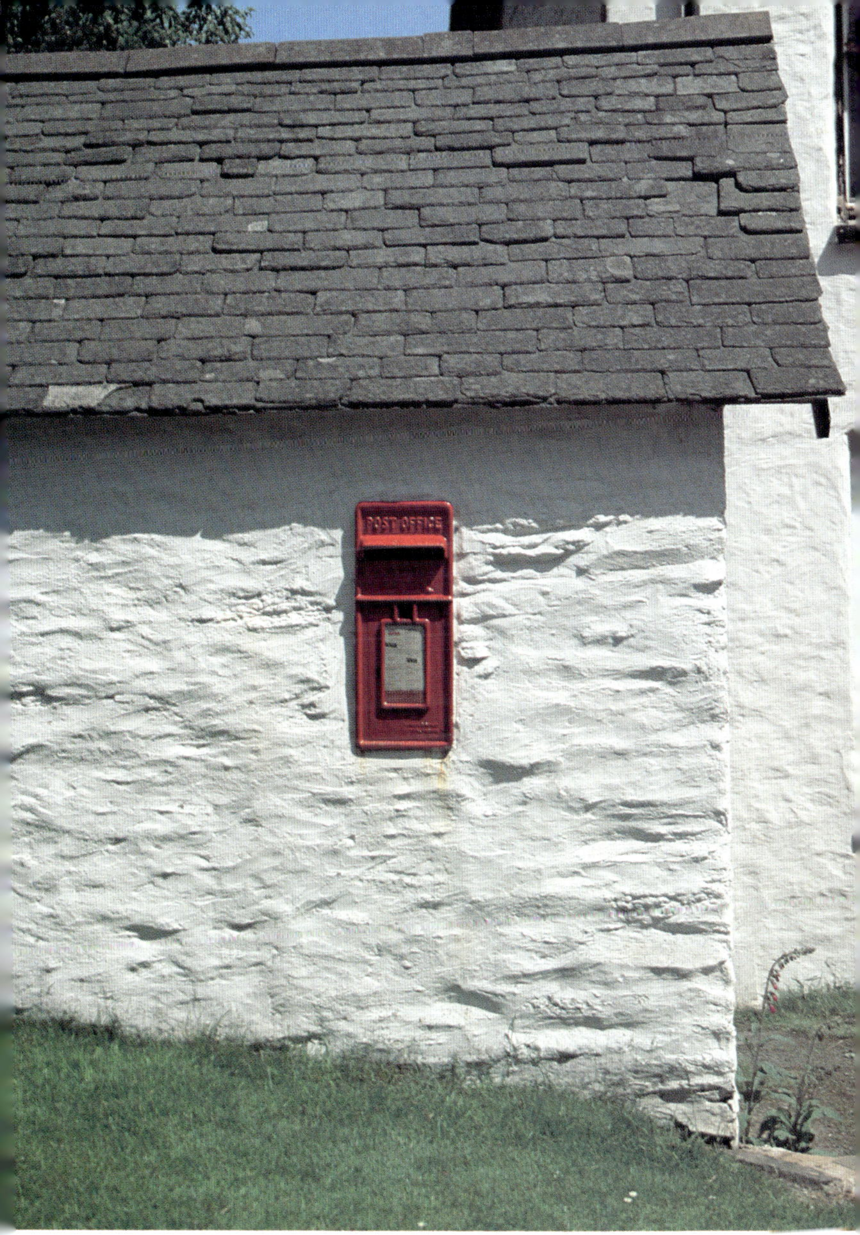

Always be on the lookout for splashes of colour. This British postbox was very eye-catching in the Welsh countryside.

Photograph: Janet Raby

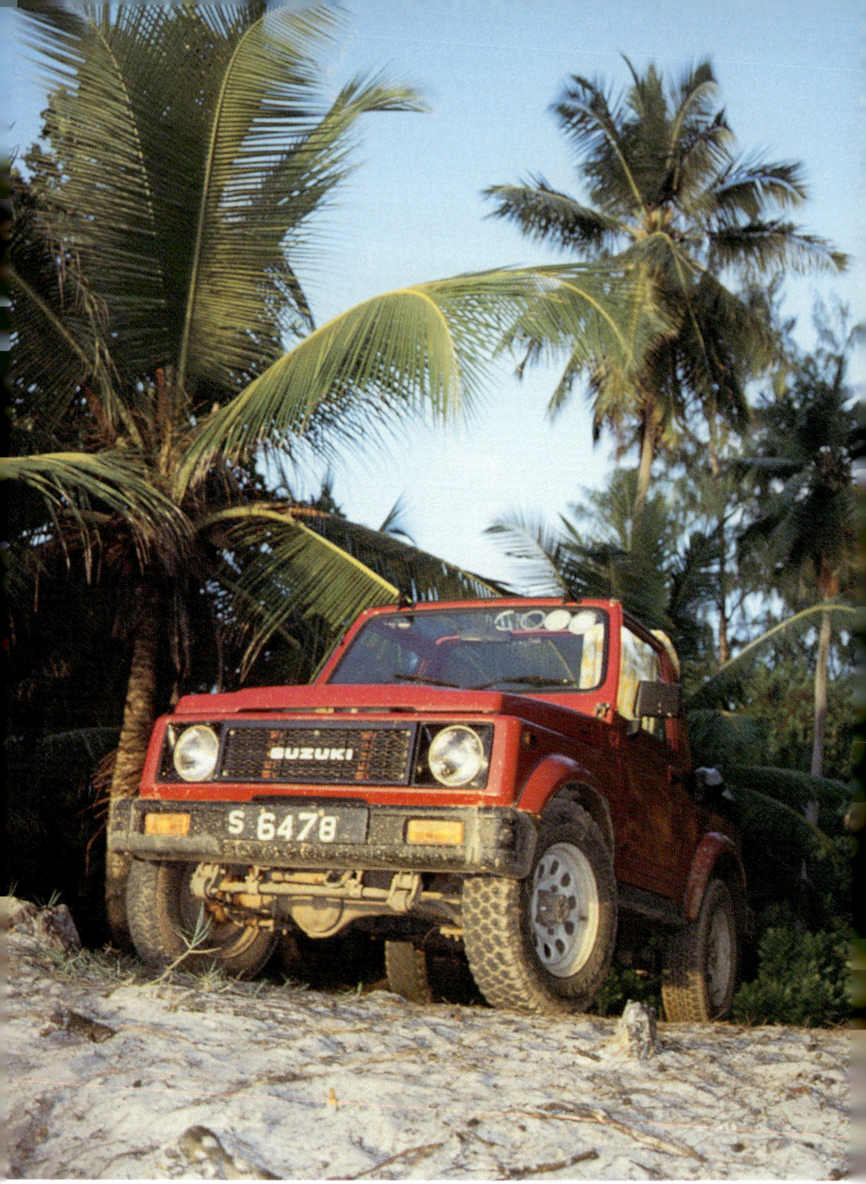

Car photographs need not be set up. The hired 4x4 was left at the top of a beach and the photo opportunity spotted on returning from a swim.

Photograph: Philip Raby

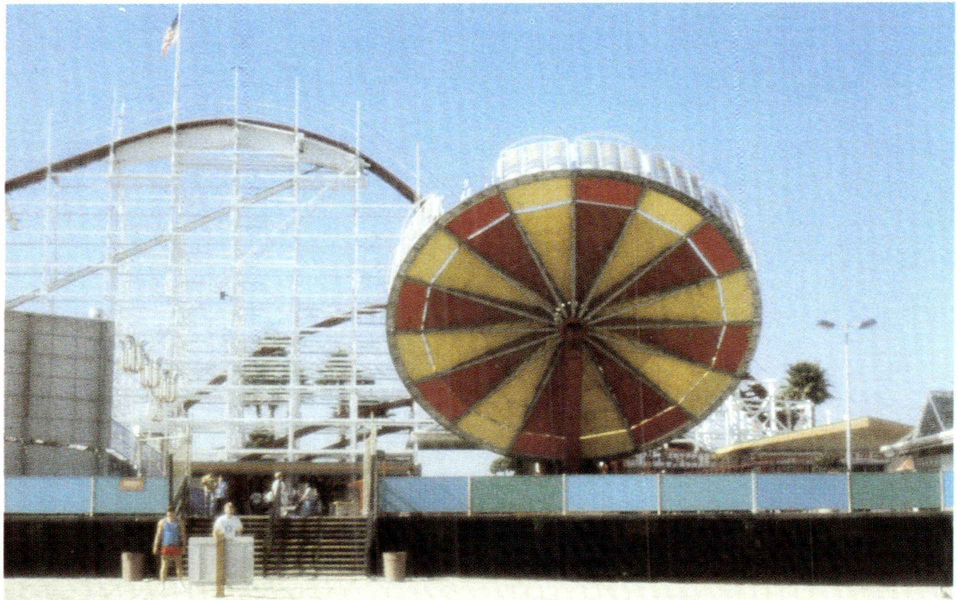

Think about composition when you take photographs. This shot of Santa Cruz funfair was photographed using the rule-of-thirds. The coloured wheel is positioned one-third of the way into the picture, giving a balanced, harmonius composition. Don't forget though, rules are made to be broken - you can also achieve stunning compositions by placing the main subject bang in the middle of the frame.

Photograph: Philip Raby

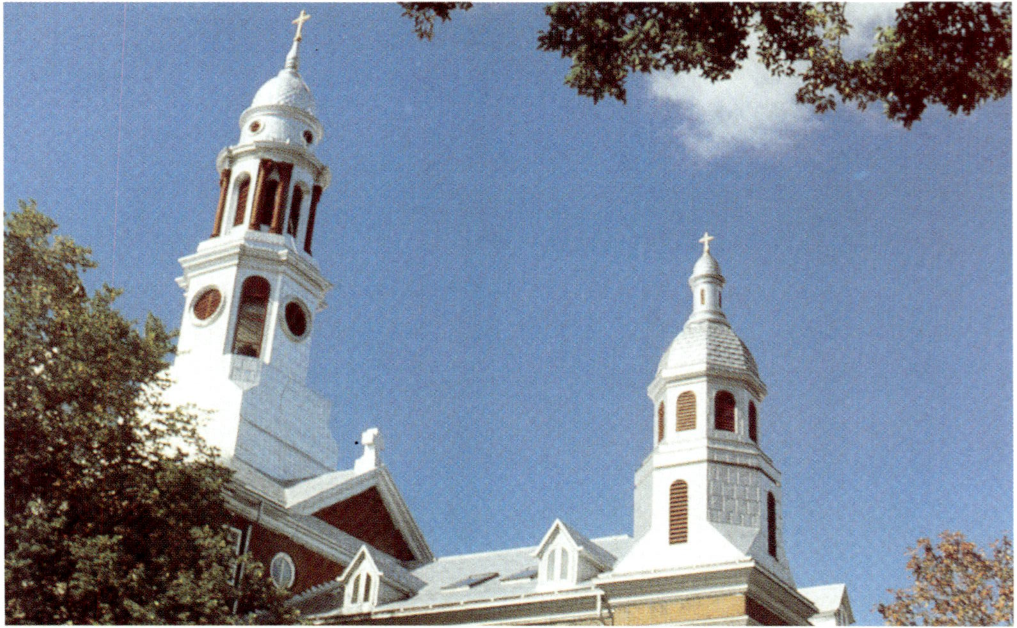

Try and make your photographs more interesting by framing them with some foreground interest. This photograph of an old building in Quebec City has been made more interesting by including the branches of trees in the bottom left and top right of the frame.

Photograph: Philip Raby

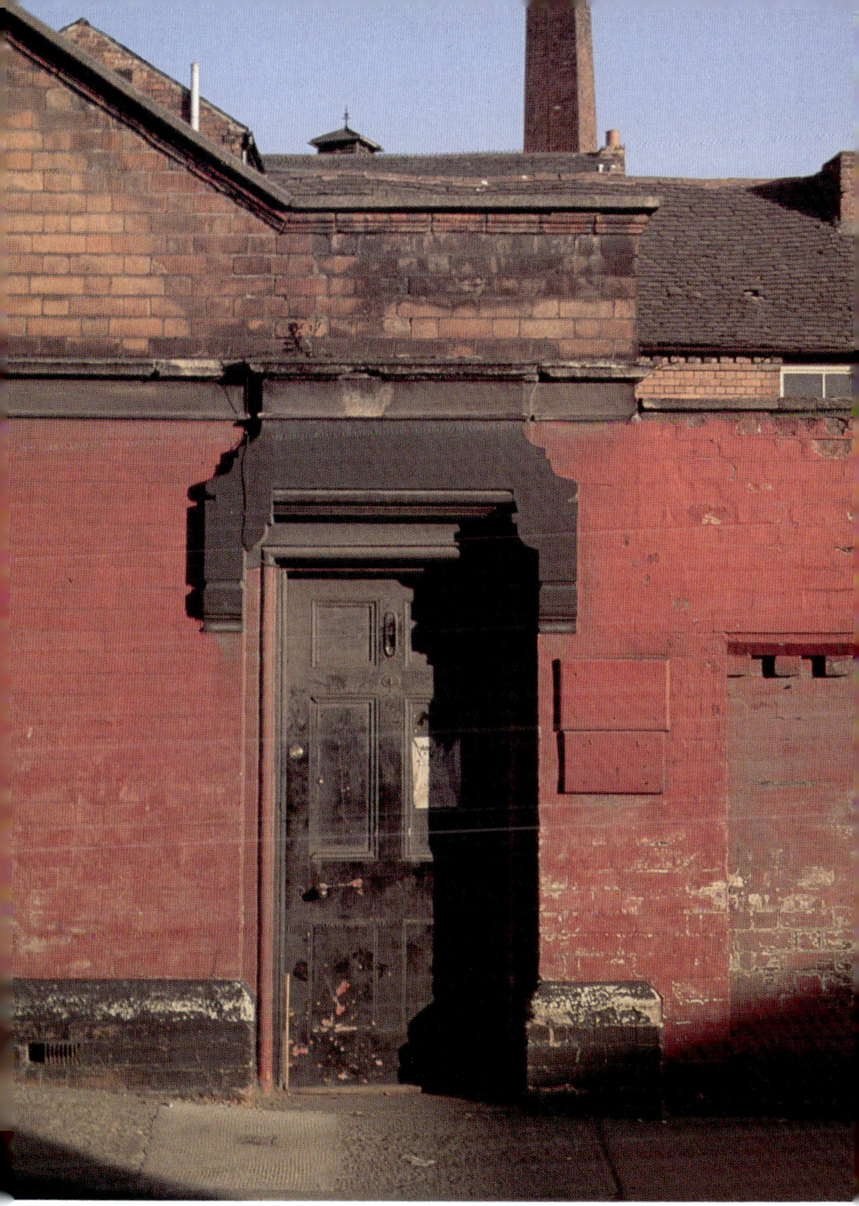

Time of day can make a great difference to your photographs. In this study of a doorway, evening light has added a warm glow to what would otherwise have been a drab scene.

Photograph: Philip Raby

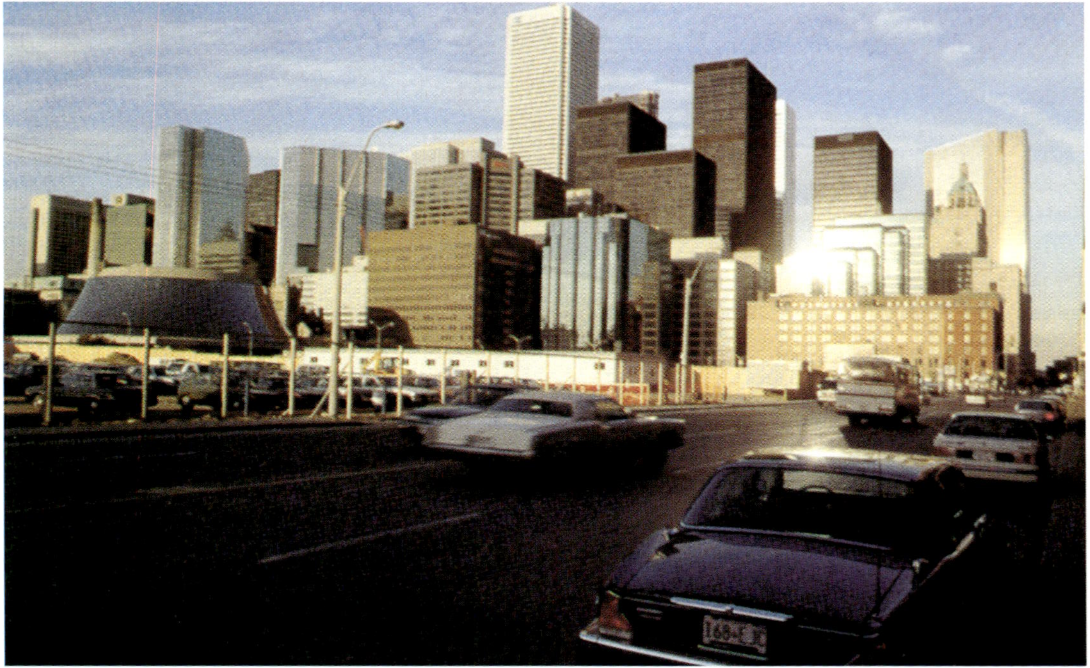

Here is another example of evening light. The low sun makes the Toronto skyline glow, while the foreground remains in shadow.

Photograph: Philip Raby

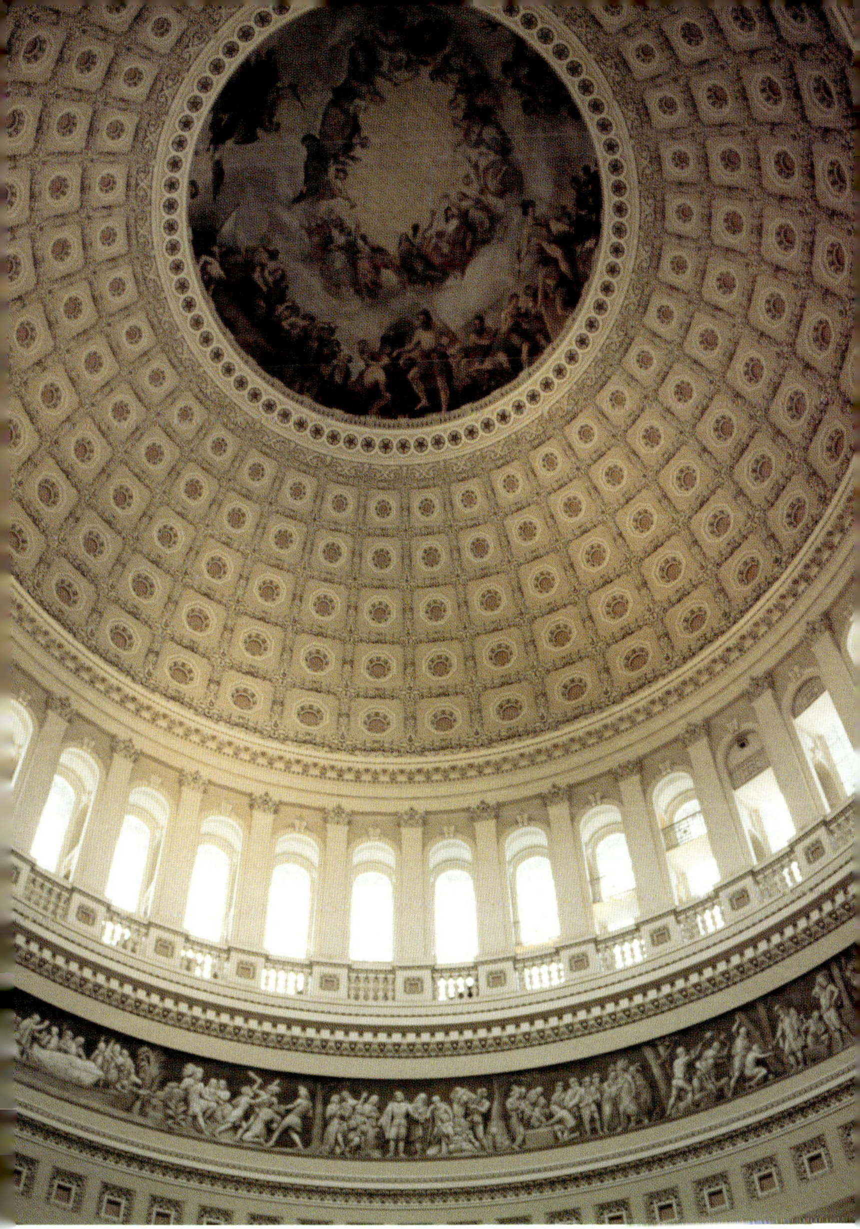

Always be on the lookout for unusual views. This is the inside of the Capitol Building in Washington DC, looking straight up.

Photograph: Philip Raby

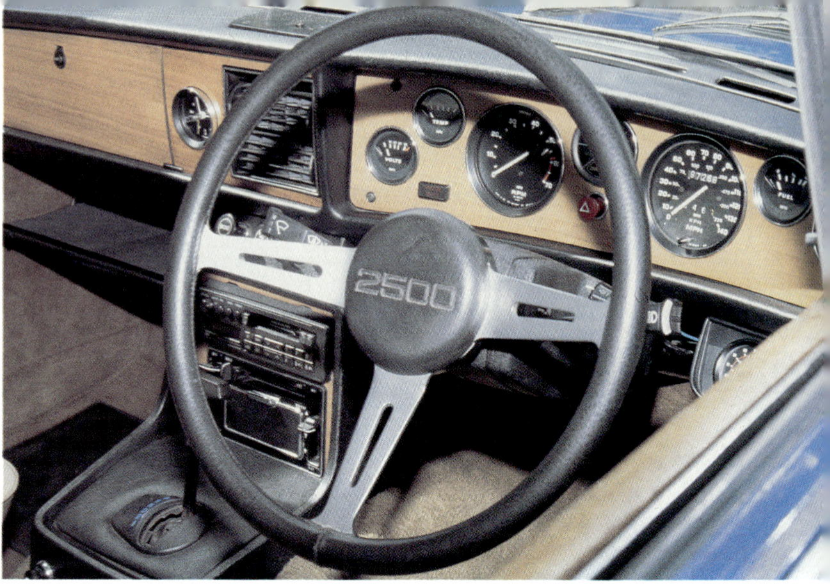

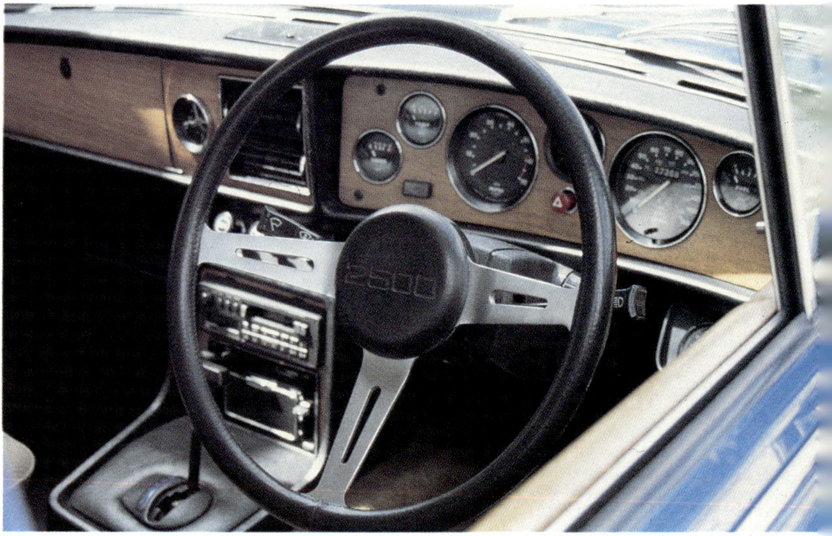

Be careful when using flash. Look at these two photographs of the interior of a classic Triumph. The top one was shot with a Speedlite 540EZ flashgun, which has caused harsh shadows to fall on the dashboard. Turning the flash off and using ambient light has created the more successful lower picture.

Photograph: Philip Raby

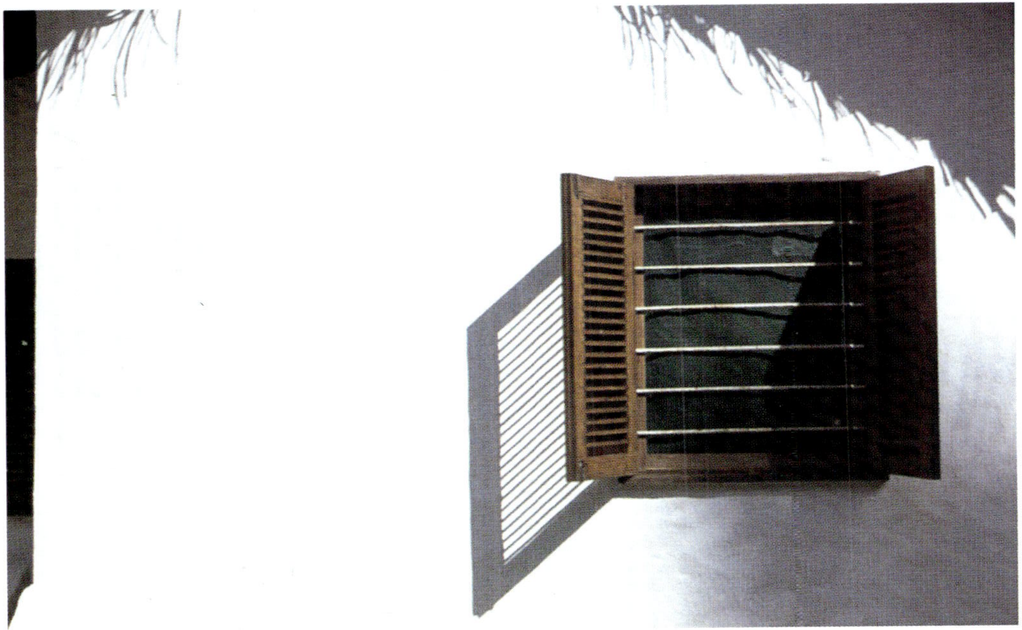

Auto Exposure Bracketing was used to take this photograph. It was thought that the white wall would confuse the camera's meter. But, surprisingly, the most successful exposure was the one suggested by the camera, which just goes to show how good evaluative metering is.

Photograph: Philip Raby

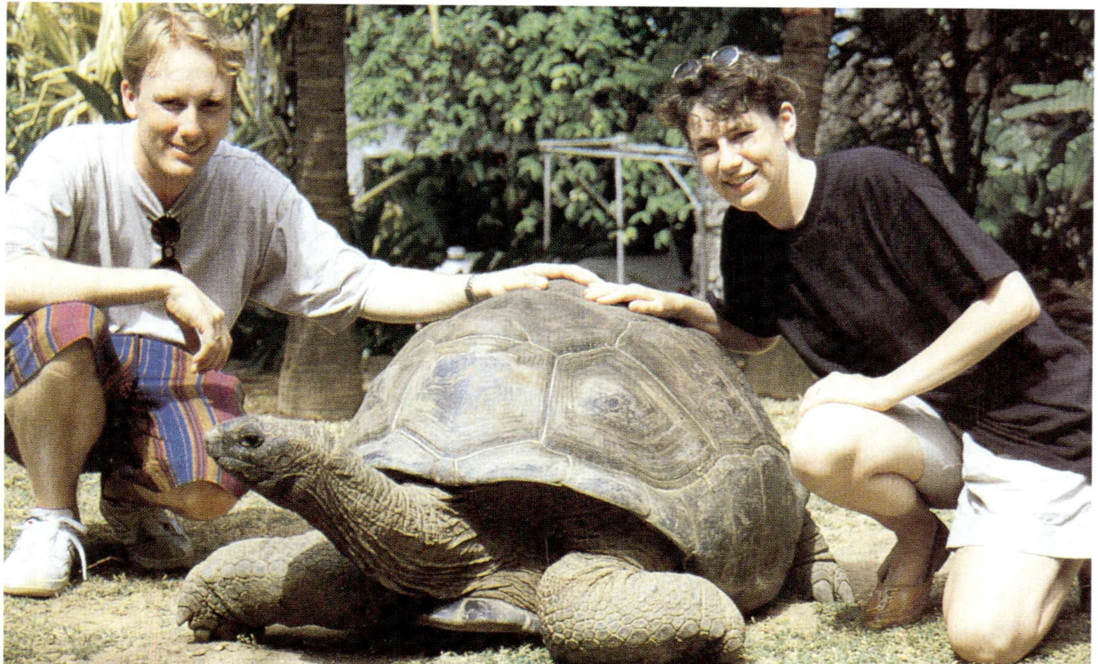

The self-timer on the EOS 50/E - Elan II/E is great for holiday snaps. Remember - in years to come, your photographs of family and friends will be the ones that you cherish most!.

Photograph: Philip Raby

You may hear people refer to a wide maximum aperture lens as fast, this is because it allows you to set a faster shutter speed than would be possible with a smaller maximum aperture lens in the same conditions. Fast lenses tend to have large front elements to allow more light to enter. They are also more expensive than slower lenses.

Some zoom lenses have a variable maximum aperture that depends on the focal length set. For instance, most standard zooms have a maximum aperture that varies from f3.5 to f5.6.

Prime and zoom lenses

Once upon a time, all lenses had a fixed focal length. Then along came zoom lenses with variable focal lengths. However, the optical quality of these early zooms left a lot to be desired and were spurned by serious photographers.

Today, zoom lenses give excellent results and are used extensively by amateurs and professional photographers alike. But they do have their drawbacks. The main one being that in most cases they do not offer such a wide maximum aperture as an equivalent fixed focal length, or prime, lens. For instance, a standard zoom lens normally has a maximum aperture range of f3.5-f5.6, while a cheap and cheerful 50mm prime lens has a maximum aperture of f1.8. If you want the ultimate standard lens, choose the incredible EF 50mm f1.0L USM lens, the world's fastest SLR camera lens.

Prime lenses still offer the best quality, but most people are unlikely to notice the difference between a picture shot on a Canon zoom and an equivalent prime lens.

Zoom lenses offer the advantage of being a number of lenses in one – an important consideration if you are planning on carrying your equipment over long distances. For most people, the convenience and versatility of zoom lenses make them the obvious choice.

L Series lenses

You will come across some Canon EF lenses with the suffix 'L' after their description. These L Series lenses offer super-high quality optics – at a price. If you demand the best, choose L Series lenses, but normal Canon EF lenses also offer excellent results.

Wide-angle prime lenses

Wide-angle lenses are those with a focal length wider than 50mm. They take in more of a scene with their wide-angle-of-view, but objects appear small and distant in the viewfinder. What's more, wide-angle lenses can create great depth-of-field, making them ideal for landscape photography. Here are just some Canon EF wide-angle prime lenses.

EF 14mm f2.8L USM

This lens has an angle-of-view of 114°, but has rectilinear characteristics. This means that, unlike a fish-eye lens, it does not distort straight lines, but offers a more natural effect. This lens is ideal for photographing interiors and other situations where space is at a premium.

EF 15mm f2.8 Fisheye

Although there is only 1mm difference between this lens and the EF 14mm f2.8L USM, it actually has a wider angle-of-view - an incredible 180°. It distorts straight lines around the edge of the frame to create an exciting and distinctive fisheye effect.

The angle-of-view of this lens is so extreme that you have to be careful that you do not include your feet in photographs! You should also be aware of tripod legs and other unwanted paraphernalia.

Think carefully before buying the EF 15mm f2.8 Fisheye lens. The extreme effects it produces have limited uses, you may be better getting the more conservative EF

14mm f2.8L USM. Some camera dealers offer a hire service so you could hire this lens when you have a specific need for it.

EF 24mm f2.8

This is a very useful lens. Its angle-of-view of 84° is not too extreme, making it suitable for general photography, but the lens can still produce exciting wide-angle effects when you want it to.

EF 28mm f1.8

Although only 4mm between this and the EF 24mm f2.8, this lens has quite different qualities. It is an ideal first wide-angle lens because of its subtle characteristics and almost natural perspective. It also has an unusually wide maximum aperture, making it useful for low light work.

EF 35mm f2

Here's a lens with a similar angle-of-view to the human eye, making it many people's choice of a 'standard' lens, instead of the more traditional 50mm focal length. It gives a very natural perspective and is useful for landscapes, group shots and interiors.

Standard lenses

As mentioned earlier, SLR cameras were once mostly sold with a 50mm standard lens. Although zoom lenses have almost taken their place, standard lenses still have their uses. Let's take a look at some.

EF 50mm f1.8 II

A superb lens for very little money. This lens is small, light and compact, yet boasts a wide maximum aperture and excellent optical quality.

EF 50mm f1.4 USM

An alternative to the EF 50mm f1.8 II with a wider maximum aperture and Ultrasonic focus motor for fast, quiet operation.

EF 50mm f1.0L USM

A specialist lens that can be identified by its huge front element, necessary for the incredible maximum aperture of f1.0. This is the world's fastest SLR camera lens and is seven times the weight of the humble EF 50mm f1.8 II. Who said 50mm lenses were dull?

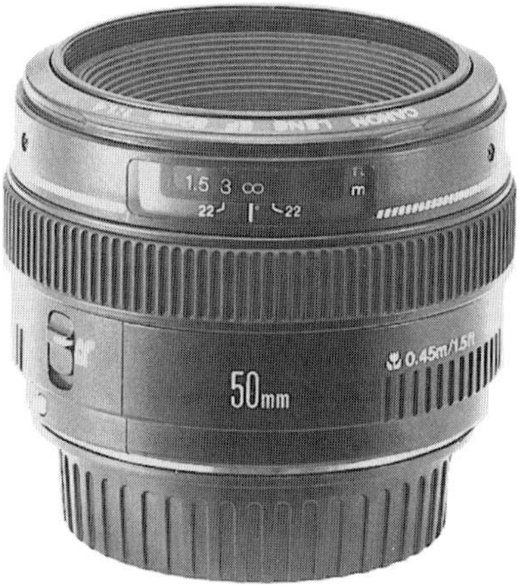

EF50mm f1.4 USM

Short telephoto lenses

Lenses with focal lengths of around 100mm are known as portrait lenses because they are ideal for taking pictures of people. Their focal length is long enough to give yourself enough distance from the subject not to intimidate them. When used at a wide aperture, these lenses throw backgrounds out-of-focus, drawing attention to the subject. Here are a few Canon short telephotos.

EF 85mm f1.2L USM

You may wonder what the point of this lens is when its focal length is covered by standard zooms. But look at that maximum aperture of f1.2 – not only is that useful for low light photography, it also allows you to reduce depth-of-field to a minimum.

EF 135mm f2.8 SF

Here's a lens that will appeal to the keen portrait photographer. Its focal length is ideal for taking pictures of people, and its wide aperture throws backgrounds out-of-focus. What's more, it features a useful soft focus facility.

Soft focus does not mean out-of-focus, but the image is softened by carefully controlled flare. The lens has a switch on its side that allows you to set one of two levels of soft focus. The '1' setting gives a subtle effect, while '2' is more extreme.

The amount of soft focus also depends on lens aperture. A wide aperture setting increases the soft focus effect, while small aperture reduce it considerably.

When you don't want the soft focus effect, you can turn it off and you are left with a superb short telephoto lens that gives pin-sharp images.

Medium telephoto lenses

When you cannot get close enough to your subject, you need a longer focal length lens. These medium telephotos are not so long that they have to be mounted on a tripod (although you should use a tripod or monopod whenever possible), yet are powerful enough to fill the frame with distant subjects.

EF 200mm f2.8L USM

200mm is a very useful focal length to have in your lens collection. This lens is light enough to hand hold and has a wide maximum aperture for low light work.

EF 300mm f4L USM

If you require a bit more pulling power, the extra focal length of this lens is useful. It is a low-cost lens and therefore only has a maximum aperture of f4. At focal lengths greater than 200mm you really should be using a tripod whenever possible.

EF 300mm f2.8L

This is a lens for professionals. It's expensive, but gives superb results and allows you to set a wide aperture to maintain a high shutter speed – essential for sports photography.

Super-telephoto lenses

When you start looking at lenses with focal lengths greater than 300mm, you're getting into the range of exotica – specialist lenses for specialist applications. Choose one of these if you are a keen sports or wildlife photographer. If you only need a long focal length occasionally, you may be better off hiring a lens when you require one.

EF 400mm f5.6L USM

This is the lowest priced super-telephoto lens. Compared with faster lenses, it is light and compact.

EF 400mm f2.8L USM

Here's a super-telephoto with a super-wide aperture. It's big and expensive, but ideal for sports photographers who need to be able to set wide apertures to keep shutter speeds high. The wide aperture combined with the long focal length also means that depth-of-field can be reduced to a minimum.

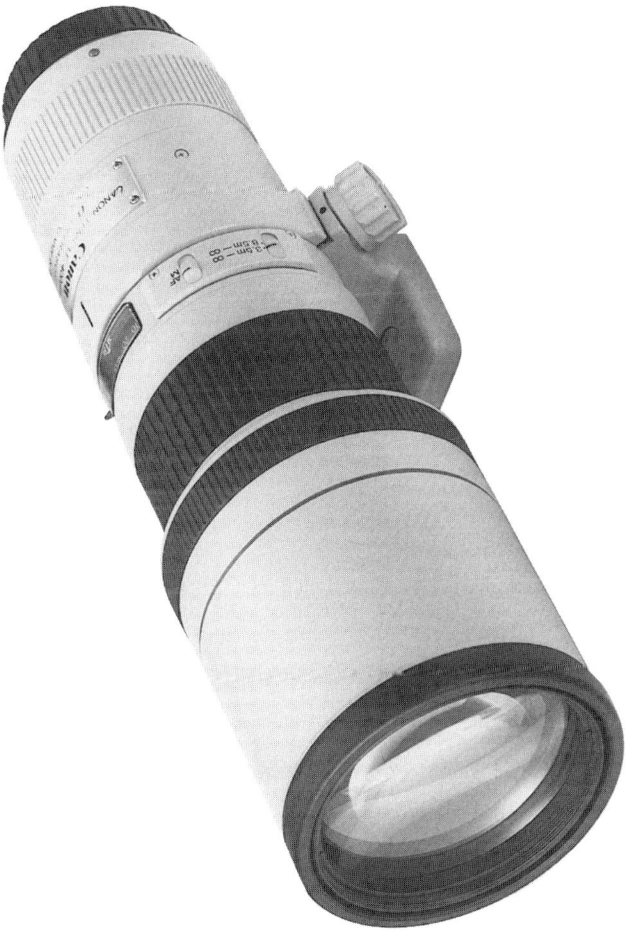

Canon Lens EF400mm f5.6L USM

EF 500mm f4.5L USM

Despite its focal length, this lens is surprisingly light and compact, making it ideal for wildlife photographers who have to carry their equipment over long distances.

EF 600mm f4L USM

This is a beast of a lens – big, expensive, and heavy. But the results from it can be incredible. A favourite lens amongst sports photographers.

EF 1200mm f5.6L USM

Here's a lens you are unlikely to buy. It costs about the same as a small house or a very nice Porsche 911 Carrera. And at 16.5kg, hand-held photography is definitely out! The lens has an angle-of-view of just 2° and its closest focusing distance is 14 metres.

1200mm not enough for you? Fit the Extender EF 2x for a super-super-telephoto of 2400mm!

If you should win the lottery, don't go to you local dealer for this lens – it is only made to special order.

Wide-angle and standard zoom lenses

As mentioned earlier, your EOS 50/E – Elan II/E probably came with a with an EF 28-80mm f3.5-5.6 III USM, a standard zoom lens that covers the most frequently used focal lengths. Here are some other wide and standard zooms.

EF 20-35mm f2.8L

This is a useful alternative to a prime wide-angle lens. It has a wide maximum aperture and a range of angle-of-views from 80° to 54°. What's more, it gives superb results at all focal lengths. An expensive lens, but worth every penny.

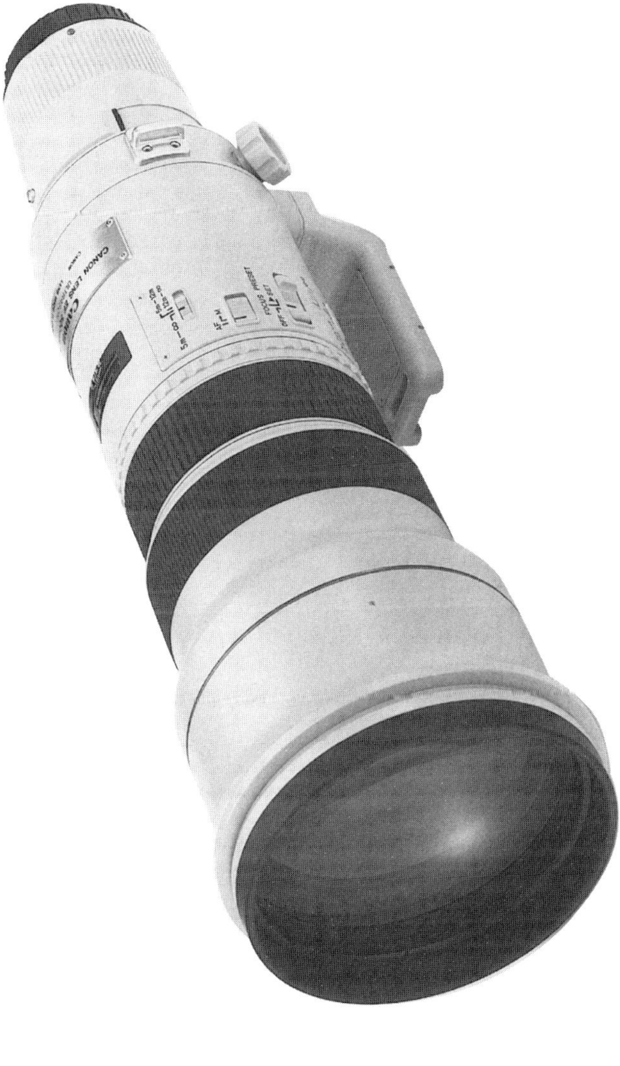

Canon Lens EF 500mm f4.5L USM

EF 35-80mm f4-5.6 USM

If you already own an EF 28-80mm f3.5-5.6 III USM, there is really no point in buying this low-cost alternative.

EF 35-80mm f4-5.6 USM

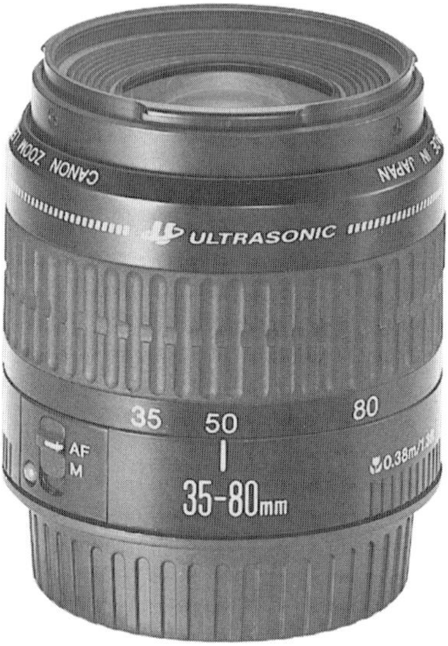

EF 28-80mm f2.8-4L USM

A luxury version of the standard zoom, this lens gives super-high quality results and has the benefit of a wide maximum aperture.

EF 28-105mm f3.5-4.5 USM

The extra range of this lens makes it worth considering as a standard zoom instead of the EF 28-80mm f3.5-5.6 III USM. At the 105mm end, it is a useful portrait lens.

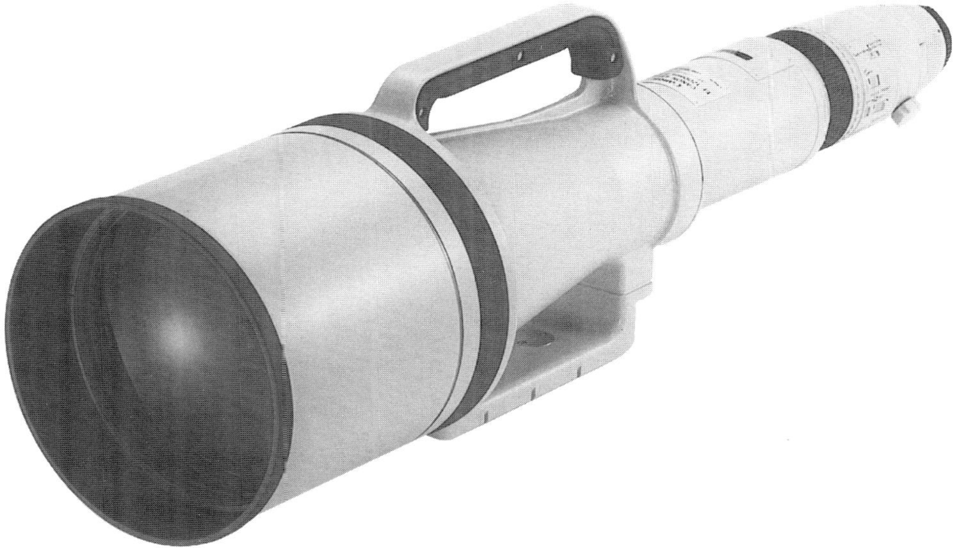

EF 1200mm f5.6L USM

Telephoto zoom lenses

A telephoto zoom lens is probably the first lens you will buy to accompany your standard zoom. Let's take a look at a few from the Canon arsenal.

EF 80-200mm f4.5-5.6 USM

A useful lens with a focal length range that follows on neatly from that of the standard zoom. This lens is superb value for money and surprisingly compact at just 78mm long.

EF 80-200mm f4.5-5.6 USM

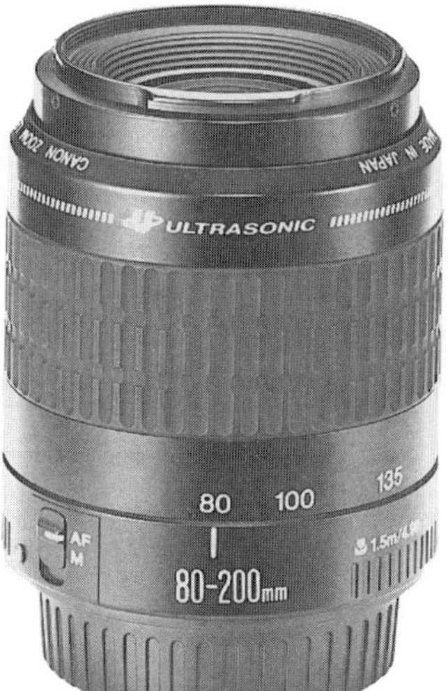

EF 100-300mm f4.5-5.6 USM

A zoom lens with a very useful range. But remember that at focal lengths greater than 200mm, a tripod is almost essential for pin-sharp photographs.

EF 75-300mm f4-5.6 USM

A lower-cost alternative to the EF 100-300 f4.5-5.6 USM. A compact, lightweight lens with a superb focal length range.

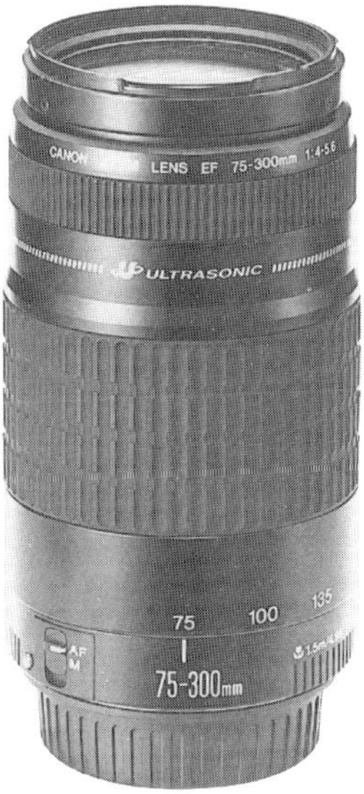

EF 75-300mm f4-5.6 USM & EF 100-300mm f4.5-5.6 USM

EF 35-350mm f3.5-5.6L USM

The ultimate zoom lens, this covers most focal lengths that you will ever need. Just think, no more carrying a bag full of lenses around with you, and no missing a vital shot because you have the wrong lens on your camera. The EF 35-350mm f3.5-5.6L is not cheap, but it could be more economical than buying a number of lenses.

This lens is not designed to be used with Canon Extenders, but it can be attached to an Extender and gives good results. However, autofocus may not operate at all focal lengths.

EF 75-300mm f4.5-5.6 IS USM

The 'IS' in the description of this lens stands for Image Stabilization. Your EOS 50/E – Elan II/E looks after focusing and exposure, so the main cause of failed photographs is camera shake. This unique lens addresses the problem.

EF 35-350mm f3.5-5.6L USM

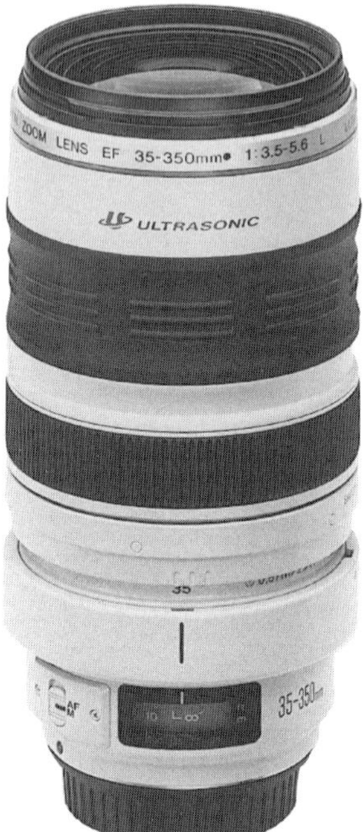

Inside the lens are two sensors that measure the amount of camera shake. This information is fed to a 16-bit microprocessor that converts the signals into drive commands for the Image-Stabilization mechanism. This is a series of coils and magnets that move a floating group of lens elements to compensate for camera shake and ensure that a steady image reaches the film.

A switch on the side of the lens allows you to switch Image Stabilization on or off. In the off position, the lens acts like any other. Image Stabilization should be turned off when the camera is used on a tripod or in the Bulb setting.

Image Stabilization does not eliminate the effect of camera shake, but it does reduce it considerably. The rule-of-thumb for hand-held photography is that the shutter speed should be no less than the inverse of the shutter speed. So if your focal length is 200mm, the shutter speed should be no longer than 1/200 second. Image Stabilization allows you to reduce this safe shutter speed by up to two stops and still get similar results.

Tilt-and-shift lenses

The axis of most cameras' lenses is at right-angles and central to the film plane, to ensure that the image is in focus and free from distortion. However, Canon produces three special lenses that have barrels that can be shifted up down, or sideways in relation to the film plane, and also tilted in any direction.

These movements allow you to control perspective, for instance to photograph a tall building without it appearing to be toppling over. They also give the facility to control depth-of-field and much more.

Canon TS-E lenses do not have focus motors – you must focus them manually. However, this is not normally a problem – tilt-and-shift photography takes time to set up, so you are unlikely to need to focus quickly.

TS-E 24mm f3.5L

A wide-angle tilt-and-shift lens for architectural and interior photography. Its wide angle-of-view can create dramatic images.

TS-E 45mm f2.8

Probably the most useful tilt-and-shift lens. Its angle-of-view gives a natural perspective, making the lens useful for architectural, still-life and other general photographic situations.

TS-E 90mm f2.8

The long focal length of this lens makes it less suitable for architectural photography – you are unlikely to be able to get far enough from most buildings to include them in the frame. However, it is an ideal lens for still-life photography because it gives a useful working distance between the camera and subject and allows you to control depth-of-field and perspective. It can also be used with Life Size Converter EF for macro photography.

Macro lenses

Macro photography opens up a whole new world. These special macro lenses allow you to get in close to your subject and still maintain sharp focus. They can also be used as conventional lenses.

EF 50mm f2.5 Compact Macro

A standard 50mm lens that focuses down to 23cm to give half life-size images. It can be fitted with Life Size Converter EF to give life-size images.

EF 100mm f2.8 Macro

A superb lens that give life-size macro images at its closest focusing distance of 31cm. The longer focal length means that there is a greater working distance between the camera and subject, which means that you are less likely to scare off insects and small animals. It also makes it easier to light the subject.

The EF 100mm f2.8 is also a useful short telephoto lens that is ideal for portraiture.

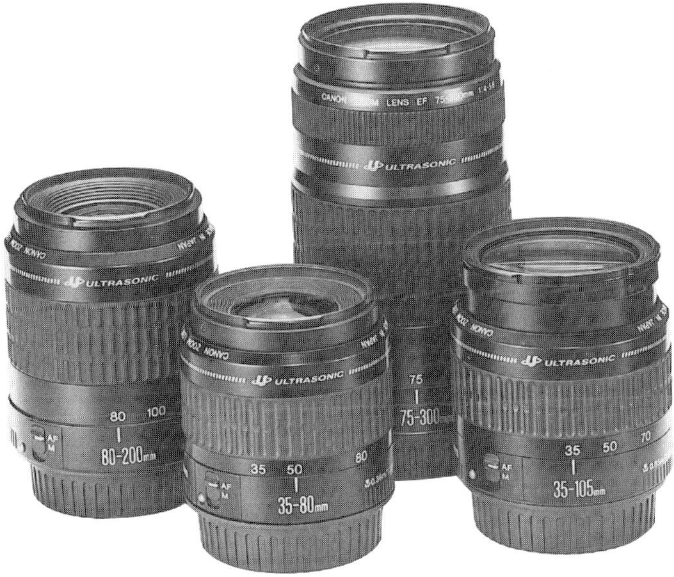

EF35-80 U, EF35-105 U
EF80-200 U, EF75-300 U

Chapter Twenty
Accessories for your EOS 50/E – Elan II/E

Your EOS 50/E – Elan II/E and standard zoom lens is a self-contained picture-taking machine that can cope with a wide range of photographic situations. However, a range of accessories is available to help you get even more from your camera. Here are just some of these.

Battery Pack BP-50

Your EOS 50/E – Elan II/E is normally powered by a compact, highly efficient 2CR5 lithium cell that fits in the camera's hand-grip. Although the 2CR5 is an ideal power supply in most situations, the batteries can normally only be bought from specialist photo and electronics dealers. You won't find one in a remote country store on a Sunday morning!

Far more readily available are AA-size pen cells, as used in radios, torches, toys and Speedlite flashguns. Battery Pack BP-50 allows you to power your EOS 50/E – Elan II/E with these versatile little cells.

The pack fits neatly onto the base of the camera and is attached via the tripod socket (there is an additional socket on the base of the pack so that you can still use the camera on a tripod). The camera's 2CR5 battery must first be removed.

As well as ordinary disposable alkaline batteries, you can also load Battery Pack BP-50 with rechargeable NiCad cells to save money and protect the environment. High power lithium AA batteries should not be used – their high initial voltage may damage the camera's electronics. Alternatively, the pack can be loaded with a single 2CR5 battery.

Not only does Battery Pack BP-50 give you an alternative choice of batteries, it also acts as a vertical holding grip. Many photographers have difficulty using their

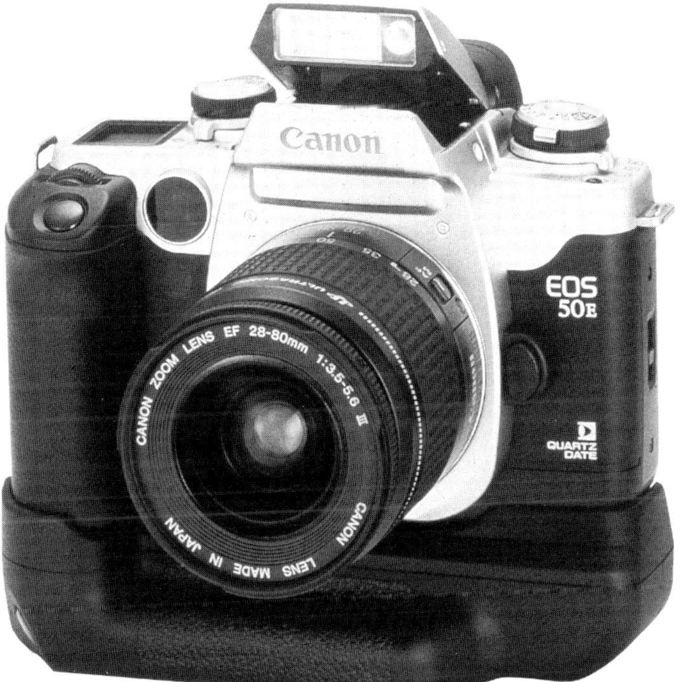

Canon EOS 50E - Elan IIE
with Battery Pack BP50

camera vertically, which is why you see so few upright, or portrait, format pictures. Battery Pack BP-50 makes the camera more comfortable to use vertically and has an auxiliary shutter button on its end so that you don't have to contort your finger around the top of the camera.

Battery Pack BP-50 will also appeal to photographers with large hands who want to make their camera a bit larger.

Battery Pack BP-5

If you need to shoot many rolls of film one after another, you will find it annoying having to keep changing the camera batteries. The solution is to use Battery Pack BP-5. This is a remote pack that clips to a belt, or carried in a pocket. It is attached to the EOS 50/E – Elan II/E by a coiled lead. This arrangement is particularly useful in very cold conditions, when the performance of batteries is impaired – the pack can be kept warm under layers of clothing.

Battery Pack BP-5 holds four D-type alkaline or rechargeable NiCad batteries. This increases tremendously the number of films that can be shot with one set of batteries.

The pack can only be used in conjunction with Battery Pack BP-50. This is because it was originally designed for the EOS 5. It has a dummy 2CR5 battery on the end of the coiled lead which joins it to the camera. This fits directly into the EOS 5, but the EOS 50/E – Elan II/E has a different shaped battery compartment that will not accept the dummy directly. The pack comes complete with a replacement battery cover for Battery Pack BP-50 that allows it to accept the coiled lead.

Remote Control RC-1

This simple, low-cost infrared controller is designed for remote firing of the camera from within about 5 metres. It is ideal for self-portraits.

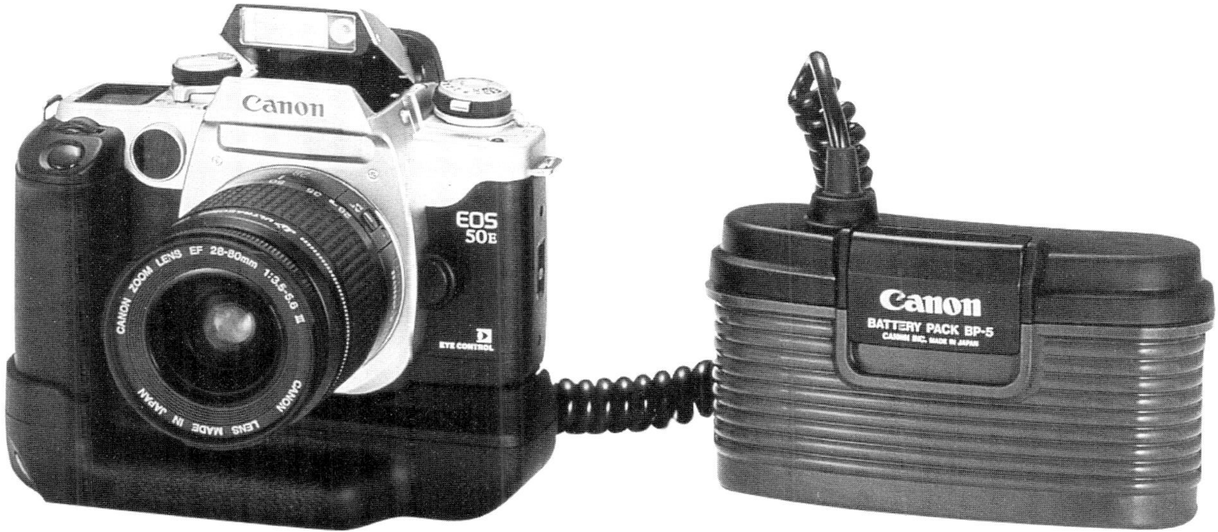

Canon EOS 50E - Elan IIE with Battery Pack BP5

Remote Switch RS-60E3

When your EOS 50/E – Elan II/E is mounted on a tripod during long exposures there is a risk that it will move as you press the shutter button to take a photograph. This movement is called camera shake and may lead to a blurred picture. One solution is to attach Remote Switch RS-60E3. This plugs into the jack socket on the right-hand end of the camera. Its 60cm lead terminates in a small hand control that has a button that duplicates the action of the camera shutter button.

Note that some other Canon EOS remote devices use a different type of plug and therefore cannot be used with the EOS 50/E – Elan II/E.

Lens accessories

Here are some accessories that allow you to do more with your Canon EF lenses.

Extension Tubes

An extension tube fits between the camera and lens to increase the lens-to-film distance and therefore allow closer focusing for macro work. Two extension tubes are available for your EOS 50/E – Elan II/E: Extension Tube EF25 which is 25mm long, and the shorter Extension Tube EF12 which is 12mm long.

Extenders

If you have an EF 70-200mm F2.8L lens or any EF telephoto prime lens with a focal length of 200mm or greater, you can use an EF Extender to increase the focal length of your lens, but with some reduction of maximum aperture.

Extender EF 1.4x increases the focal length by 1.4x and reduces the maximum aperture by 1 stop.

Extender EF 2x doubles the focal length but decreases the aperture by 2 stops.

An Extender can be used with the EF 35-350mm f3.5-5.6L USM, but autofocus may not be possible at all focal lengths.

Close-up lenses

These inexpensive accessories fit onto the front of your EF lens in the same way as a filter. In fact, they are often incorrectly called 'close-up filters' but they do not filter the light in any way.

What a close-up lens does is act like a magnifying glass, allowing you to focus much closer than normal and fill the frame with small objects. Because it does not reduce the amount of light that reaches the film, a close-up lens is an ideal introduction to macro photography.

Canon produces three close-up lenses – 500, 250D and 500D. Close-up Lens 500 is a low-cost item, but it still gives very good results. Close-up Lenses 250D and 500D have a double element design and offer higher image quality.

Lens hoods

One of the simplest and cheapest ways that you can improve your photographs is to use a lens hood. Canon produces lens hoods for most of its EF lenses and your photo dealer will be able to supply the correct one for your lens.

A lens hood reduces stray light from falling on the surface of the lens. This light is non image-forming and will cause flare which in turn degrades the image.

Dioptric Correction Lenses

Very few people have perfect eyesight, most of us are either short-sighted or long-sighted to some degree. However, the viewfinder of your EOS 50/E – Elan II/E is calibrated for people with good eyesight. You may find that you can use the camera happily with your spectacles on, but some people find this awkward. It all depends on your particular eyes and the shape of your spectacles.

If you have trouble using spectacles with your camera, you can fit a correction lens to your EOS 50/E – Elan II/E. A range of correction lenses is available with their strengths indicated in dioptres, from -4 dioptres to +3 dioptres. The positive strengths are for long-sightedness and the minus ones for short-sighted people.

Two types of correction lens are available for EOS cameras. Dioptric Correction Lenses 'E' fit most EOS models including the EOS 50/E – Elan II/E, although Eye-control Focus may not be possible. If you own an EOS 50E – Elan IIE you should use the Dioptric Correction Lenses Ed, which are designed for use with EOS Eye-control cameras.

Remember to remove your spectacles when using an EOS with a Dioptric Correction Lens attached.

Camera Case EH9-L

A few years ago, everyone had an 'every-ready' case for their SLR camera. But they were not convenient to use and fell out of favour, being christened 'never-ready cases'!

However, Canon produces one for those photographers who like to keep their EOS 50/E – Elan II/E protected. Camera Case EH9-L accepts the camera with an EF 28-80mm f3.5-5.6 III USM or EF 28-105mm f3.5-4.5 USM lens attached.

Chapter Twenty One

Jargon buster – A glossary of EOS terms

If you thought that Fill-in Ratio control was something to do with plastering, and a PC lead was a non-racist, non-sexist contact, then you'd better read this glossary of EOS terms.

A-TTL
See Advanced TTL

Accessory shoe
See hotshoe

Advanced TTL
Normally called A-TTL. A through-the-lens (TTL) flash metering system unique to EOS cameras and Speedlites. It allows the camera and flash to work together to calculate the best shutter speed and aperture for a correct flash and daylight exposure.

AEB
See Auto Exposure Bracketing.

AFD
Short for Arc Form Drive, a focusing motor used in early Canon EF lenses.

AI Servo
A focus mode of the EOS 50/E – Elan II/E that continually tracks moving subjects.

Aperture
An adjustable hole formed by the lens diaphragm to limit the amount of light that reaches the lens.

Aperture Priority mode
A shooting mode that allows the photographer to choose the lens aperture.

Auto Exposure Bracketing
A feature of the EOS 50/E – Elan II/E that allows you to take three photographs each at a slightly different exposure.

Auxiliary Focusing Light
A light on the front of the EOS 50/E – Elan II/E to aid focusing in low light.

BASIS
Short for Base Stored Image Sensor, part of the EOS 50/E – Elan II/E autofocus system.

Battery
The power cells that provide the EOS 50/E – Elan II/E with electricity. The standard battery is a 2CR5, although readily-available AA or D-type batteries can be fitted in optional external packs.

Built-in flash
The pop-up flash unit of the EOS 50/E – Elan II/E.

Bulb
A shutter speed setting available in Manual. When this is set, the shutter remains open as long as the shutter button is held down.

Canon
Manufacturer of cameras, lenses and accessories. Derived from the Buddhist name, Kwannon, it was changed to Canon in 1935 to avoid offending religious groups, and to sound more acceptable to Western ears. Both names are pronounced the same by the Japanese.

Centre-weighted Average metering
A metering system that takes a light reading from the whole image, but with an emphasis on the central area.

Close-up mode
A PIC mode for photographing near objects.

Command Dial
The dial on the top of the EOS 50/E – Elan II/E that allows the shooting mode to be set. Also locks the camera when not in use.

Continuous
A winding mode of the EOS 50/E – Elan II/E that allows a number of frames to be shot while the shutter button is held down.

Custom functions
A feature of the EOS 50/E – Elan II/E that allows users to alter some of the camera settings to suit their way of working.

Depth-of-field preview
A facility on the EOS 50/E – Elan II/E that allows the aperture to be closed down prior to firing the shutter to see the amount of depth-of-field.

Depth mode
A shooting mode that allows the photograph to define how much of the image appears sharp.

Dioptric correction lens
An optional lens that fits over the viewfinder that corrects for eyesight deficiencies. A range of different strength lenses is available.

DX Coding
A system of coding used on most 35mm film cassettes. The EOS 50/E – Elan II/E reads this code to enable the correct film speed to be set.

EF lens mount
The lens mount used by the EOS 50/E – Elan II/E and all other EOS models

Electronic Input Dial
A rotary dial behind the shutter button of the EOS 50/E – Elan II/E. Used to set camera functions such as shutter speed and aperture.

EOS
The name of Canon autofocus SLR cameras. Short for Electro Optical System and pronounced as one word – ee-os, not E.O.S..

Evaluative metering
The standard metering system of the EOS 50/E – Elan II/E. The scene is divided into six segments and light readings taken from each section to ensure correct exposure in difficult lighting situations.

Evaluative TTL
Normally called E-TTL. A flash metering mode used by the EOS 50/E – Elan II/E and Speedlite 380EX that utilises the camera's Evaluative metering system.

Exposure Compensation
A feature of the EOS 50/E – Elan II/E that allows the exposure to be increased or decreased by a chosen amount.

Eye-control Focus
A feature of the EOS 50E – Elan IIE that senses which focus point the user's eye is looking at.

Fill-in Ratio Control
See Flash Exposure Compensation.

First curtain sync
The standard way that a Speedlite or built-in flash is synchronised to the camera shutter. The flash fires immediately the shutter is fully open.

Flash Exposure Compensation
A feature on the EOS 50/E – Elan II/E that allows the balance of the ambient and flash exposures to be altered. Also called Fill-in Ratio Control.

Focal plane
The film plane inside the camera. The EOS 50/E – Elan II/E uses focal plane shutter – it is directly in front of the film.

Focusing screen
Also known as a viewing screen. An opaque plastic screen inside the EOS 50/E – Elan II/E that light is deflected onto from the lens to form an image.

Focusing ring
A knurled ring found on some EF lenses to allow manual focusing when the lens is set to Manual focus.

Full Auto
A simple-to-use shooting mode that turns the EOS 50/E – Elan II/E into a point-and-shoot camera.

Function button
A button on the back of the EOS 50/E – Elan II/E that sets little used features.

Guide Number
An indication of the power of a flashgun. By dividing by the flash-to-subject distance, it is possible to calculate the aperture to set for a correct exposure during manual flash photography. Can be quoted in either feet or metres and normally assumes the use of ISO 100 film

Hotshoe
Fitting on top of the EOS 50/E – Elan II/E that accepts a Speedlite or other accessories. It has electrical contacts that electronically link the camera and flash.

Landscape mode
A PIC mode for photographing scenery.

Liquid crystal display (LCD)
An electronic device that becomes black when an electronic charge is passed through it. The LCD panel on the EOS 50/E – Elan II/E displays information about camera settings.

Lock
A setting on the EOS 50/E – Elan II/E that turns off the camera and prevents the shutter from firing.

Macro Ring Lite
A Canon ring flash that attaches to the front of the lens and gives even illumination for macro photography. Often incorrectly called Macro Lite.

Manual mode
A shooting mode that leaves the photographer to set both the aperture and the shutter speed.

Multiple exposures
A feature of the EOS 50/E – Elan II/E that allows more than one exposure to be made on a single frame of film.

Off camera flash
A technique using a flashgun not mounted on the camera hotshoe.

Off Camera Shoe Cord
A Canon accessory that allows a single Speedlite to be used a short distance away from the EOS 50/E – Elan II/E while retaining all dedicated functions.

One shot
A focus mode of the EOS 50/E – Elan II/E that focuses once and then locks the focus setting.

Op/Tech
The world's most comfortable camera strap.

Partial metering
A metering system that takes a light reading just from the central 9.5% of the image area.

PC lead
A simple two-core lead used to connect a camera to a non-dedicated flashgun.

PC/hotshoe adaptor
Allows a PC lead to be connected to the EOS 50/E – Elan II/E, which does not have a PC socket.

PIC modes
See Program Image Control.

Portrait mode
A PIC mode for photographing people.

Program Image Control
Commonly known as PIC modes, these are easy-to-use settings that customise the EOS 50/E – Elan II/E to suit specific photographic subjects.

Program mode
A shooting mode where the camera sets both the shutter speed and the aperture, but the photograph can override some settings.

Program Shift
A feature that allows the photographer to alter the settings made by the EOS 50/E – Elan II/E in Program mode while retaining a correct exposure.

Quartz Date (QD)
A version of the EOS 50/E – Elan II/E with a facility for the time or date to be imprinted onto the film.

Quick Control Dial
A dial on the back of the EOS 50/E – Elan II/E that allows certain settings to be made quickly and easily with the right thumb.

Red-eye reduction
A light shone at the subject by the EOS 50/E – Elan II/E during built-in flash photography. It helps to reduce the risk of red-eye – a distinctive effect caused by light from a direct flash entering a subject's eyes and bouncing off red blood vessels behind the retina.

Reflex mirror
A mirror inside the EOS 50/E – Elan II/E that deflects light that has passed through the lens onto the focusing screen.

Remote control
An accessory that allows you to control the EOS 50/E – Elan II/E from a distance. Also used to avoid camera shake.

Second curtain sync
A setting on some Speedlites that causes the flash to fire just before the shutter closes, instead of immediately the shutter is fully open.

Self-timer
A setting on the EOS 50/E – Elan II/E that delays the firing of the shutter for ten seconds after pressing the shutter button.

Shutter
A blind in the camera that opens for a preset time to allow light to reach the film.

Shutter button
This button is pressed to take a photograph.

Shutter Priority mode
A shooting mode that allows the photographer to choose the shutter speed.

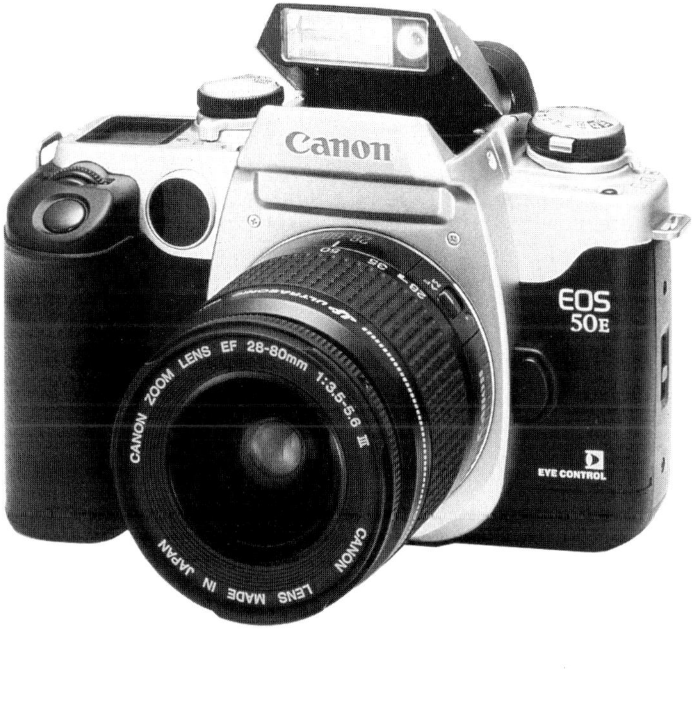

Canon EOS 50E - Elan IIE

Single
A winding mode of the EOS 50/E – Elan II/E that takes one photograph each time that the shutter button is pressed.

SLR
Short for Single Lens Reflex, the EOS 50/E – Elan II/E is an SLR camera. A mirror and prism deflect light passing through the lens to the focusing screen so that what you see in the viewfinder is the same image that the film is exposed to when the shutter button is pressed.

Speedlite
The brand-name of Canon electronic flashguns.

Sport mode
A PIC mode for photographing action.

Sto-Fen
'Softie' flash diffuser to reduce the risk of red-eye, harsh shadows and reflections during flash photography with a Speedlite.

Stop-down metering
The metering system found on the EOS 50/E – Elan II/E that allows non-dedicated lenses and accessories to be used.

Sync speed
The maximum shutter speed that can be used for flash photography on a camera with a focal plane shutter. The sync speed of the EOS 50/E – Elan II/E is 1/125 second.

Through-the-lens
See TTL metering.

TTL metering
Short for through-the-lens. A meter inside the camera body measures light that has passed through the lens.

USM
Short for Ultrasonic Motor, a fast, silent focusing motor used in Canon EF lenses.

Viewfinder
The eyepiece at the back of the EOS 50/E – Elan II/E that you look through to see the image.

Chapter Twenty Two
Specifications

Viewfinder coverage: 90% horizontal, 92% vertical.

Focusing screen: New Laser-matte screen, non-interchangeable.

Shutter: Electronically controlled vertical-travel focal plane shutter.

Shutter speeds: 1/4000 to 30 seconds plus Bulb. Can be set in 1/2 step increments.

X sync: 1/125 second (flash sync at all speeds when using Speedlite 380EX).

AF control system: TTL-CT-SIR (Through-The-Lens Cross Type Secondary Image Registration) phase-detection type using BASIS (Base Stored Image Sensor).

AF modes: One-shot AF, AI Servo with Predictive AF, AI Focus (switches automatically between One Shot and AI Servo). Manual focus possible.

Focusing points: Three points provided. Can be set by camera or user. EOS 50E – Elan IIE also offers Eye-control point selection.

AF working range: EV 0-18 at ISO 100.

Light metering: TTL full aperture metering using a 6-zone SPC (Silicon Photo Cell). Three metering patterns available: 6-zone evaluative metering; centre-weighted average metering; partial metering (approx. 9.5% of image area) at centre of screen or linked to focus point.

Metering range: EV 1 to 20.

Film speed range: ISO 6 to 6400 (set by user); ISO 25 to 5000 (set by DX).

Shooting modes: Full Auto; Portrait; Landscape; Close-up; Sports; Shutter Priority AE; Aperture Priority AE; Depth-of-Field AE; Intelligent Program AE; E-TTL, A-TTL and TTL Program Flash AE; Manual; Bulb.

Exposure compensation: ±2 stops in 1/2 step increments.

Auto Exposure Bracketing (AEB): ±2 stops in 1/2 step increments.

Multiple exposure: up to 9 can be preset.

Depth-of-field preview: with Eye-control (EOS 50E – Elan IIE only) or Custom Function.

Film loading: Automatic.

Film wind: Automatic; single or continuous exposure.

Maximum winding speed: approximately 2.5 fps.

Film rewind: Automatic. Silent mode approximately 12 seconds with 24-exposure film; highspeed rewind approximately 6 seconds with 24-exposure film (mode set by Custom Function). Mid-roll rewind possible.

Power source: One 6 volt lithium 2CR5. Optional Battery Pack BP-5 and Battery Pack BP-50 available.

Custom Functions: 11 available.

Built-in flash: Range 1-4.6m (ISO 100 f2.8).

Flash contacts: Hotshoe.

Flash compensation: Up to ±2 stops in 1/2 step increments. Possible with both built-in flash and external Speedlite.

Remote control: 2.5mm jack socket. Wireless remote sensor for Remote Controller RC-1

Self-timer: 10 second delay.

Size: 153 x 105 x 71mm

Weight: 590g.

Introduced: August 1995

COMPLETE

Canon

USER'S GUIDE

SPEEDLITES

420EZ 430EZ 540EZ

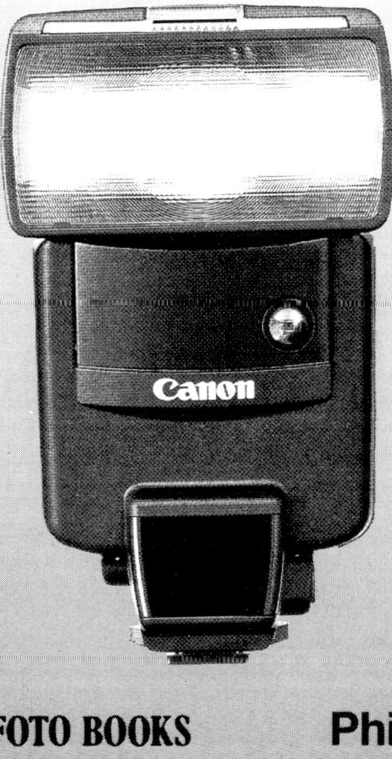

FEATURES Speedlite 300TL

AN ORIGINAL

HOVE FOTO BOOKS

Philip Raby

ACCESSORIES WELL WORTH LOOKING AT!

OP/TECH

The world's most comfortable cameras, bag and tripod straps (binoculars too). Op/tech has a built-in weight reduction system that makes equipment feel 50% lighter and 100% more comfortable. From the famous 'Pro-Camera Strap' to the 'Bag Strap' and the 'Tripod Strap', the style, colours and comfort which along with the non-slip grip, ensure that you have a wonderful combination of comfort and safety.

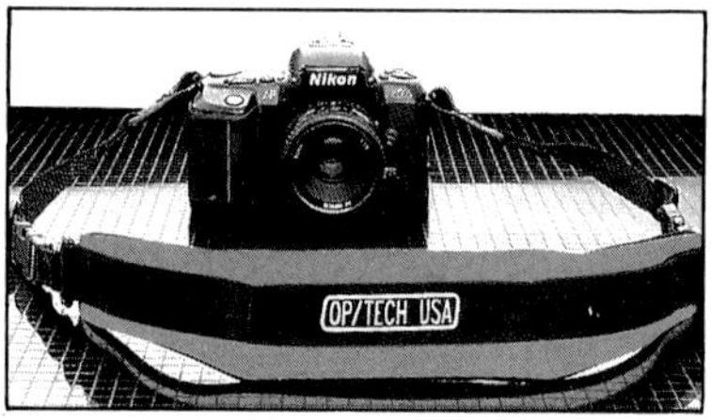

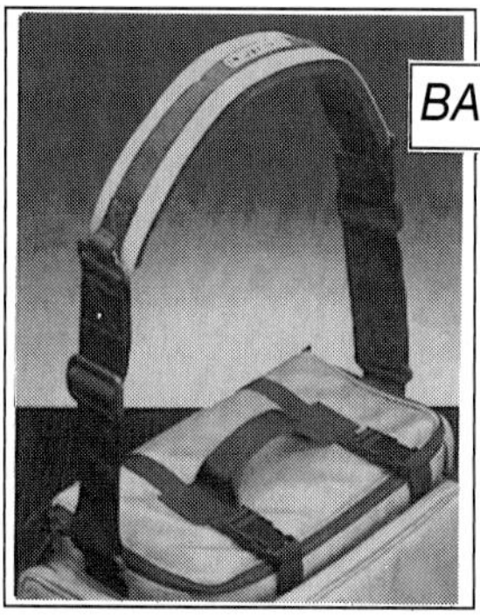

BAG STRAP

The **OP/TECH USA Bag Strap** is the answer to the problem of carrying a heavy bag for extended periods of time. By combining the patented weight reduction system with the Non Slip Grip™, you have the perfect strap for camera/video bags and cases as well as garment bags. Adjustable from 29" to 52", this strap is one of a kind. You will feel the difference!

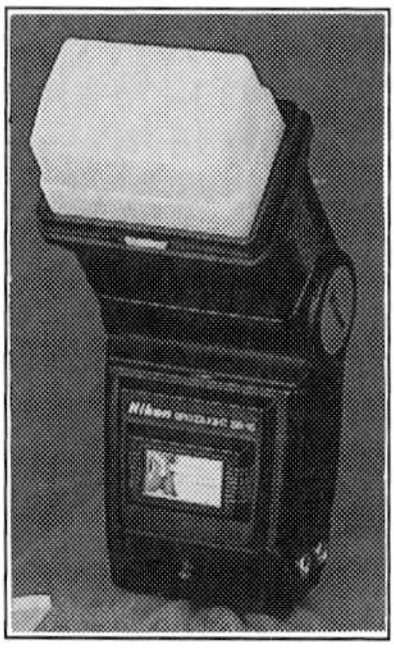

STO-FEN

The ultimate lightweight diffuser system for high powered modern flashguns. Sto-Fen offers the 'Omni-Bounce' for overall soft diffusion – often called the "softie" – which weighs in at just 15 grams and the 'Two-Way' Bounce Card for those who prefer to direct diffused light from their flash. The 'Two-Way' only weighs 25 grams, so it adds almost nothing to the overall weight of the flash. Sto-Fen are the lightest weight, most effective flash diffuser products on the market today.

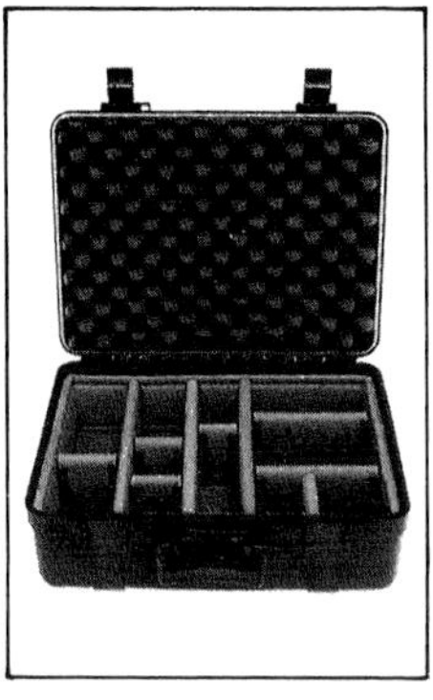

PELI-PELICAN CASES

Watertight and airtight to 30 feet for the ultimate in protection. Constructed of light weight space age structural resin with a neoprene "O" ring seal and exclusive purge valve. Supplied complete with pre-scored pick n'pluck foam or padded dividers. Also includes locking flanges, massive multiple latches for absolute security and best of all, a comfortable molded grip handle.